JESUS
THE TEACHER

BY J. M. PRICE

Former Director, School of Religious Education
Southwestern Baptist Theological
Seminary

FORT WORTH, TEXAS

CONVENTION PRESS

Nashville, Tennessee

Code number: Church Study Course for Teaching and Training
This book is number 1741 in category 17, section A

Library of Congress Catalog Card Number: 46-8509

Printed in the United States of America
55. JN 60 R.R.D.

To My Children

ELIZABETH, JOHN, JOE, JIM

with

A FATHER'S PRAYER

About the Author

JOHN MILBURN PRICE was born and reared on a farm near Fair Dealing, Kentucky. He attended the ungraded country school at Maple Springs and received the Common School Diploma through a county examination. He graduated from Western Kentucky State College with the B.S. degree.

Converted at fourteen, J. M. Price joined the Pleasant Hope Baptist Church. His teaching experience began at Cleveland school, better known as "Shoo Fly." Later he was principal of the high school at Marlow, Indian Territory.

Further education included the A.B. degree from Baylor University; the A.M. degree from Brown University; and the Th.M, Th.D, and Ph.D. degrees from Southern Baptist Theological Seminary. Baylor conferred on him the LL.D. degree. Other study was done at Mercer University, University of Dubuque, University of Chicago, and Boston University.

Dr. Price has served as pastor in Kentucky, Rhode Island, and Texas, twenty-one years with one country church. The first associational Sunday school work in the Southern Baptist Convention was done by him in the Blood River (Kentucky) Association. He was field Sunday school worker in the mountains of Kentucky for one summer and later served as state Sunday school secretary. He established the School of Religious Education at Southwestern Seminary in 1915, and directed it for more than forty years.

Dr. Price has traveled extensively in Canada, Central America, Europe, Palestine, Egypt, Asia, Australia, and Hawaii. He has written numerous books: *Christianity and Social Problems, Personal Factors in Character Building, Vital Problems in Christian Living,* and *Jesus the Teacher* (translated into Chinese, Spanish, and Portuguese). He served as general editor of *An Introduction to Religious Education, Baptist Leaders in Religious Education, Ten Men from Baylor,* and *Southwestern Men and Messages.* He was joint author of *A Survey of Religious Education,* and contributed a chapter each to *The Baptist Pulpit Speaks* by Ellis and *The Quest of God Through Understanding* by Lotz.

Dr. Price married Mabel Falk of Oklahoma, and they have four children: Elizabeth, John, Joe, and Jim.

iv

Contents

Foreword

THIS BOOK is the outgrowth of classwork in religious education at Southwestern Seminary and of addresses delivered to Sunday school teachers in churches and associational meetings and at state and Convention-wide assemblies and clinics.

It does not attempt an exhaustive or scholarly presentation of Jesus as a teacher. Rather the purpose has been to draw from his life and teaching those truths that will give vision and impetus to the rank and file of teachers.

The study grows out of the feeling that Sunday school teachers are the greatest force for good today, that they work under serious difficulties and discouragements, and that they need inspiration as well as information for their tasks.

The quotations from the New Testament are from the Revised Standard Version, copyrighted 1946, by the International Council of Religious Education and are used by permission.

Thanks are due to the various publishers for permission to quote, also to those who have read the manuscript and given criticisms and encouragement. May the book be a blessing to teachers and to other church workers everywhere.

J. M. PRICE

Some Projected Visual Materials

For Use in Teaching this Book

Filmstrips from the *Teacher Improvement Series* are listed for use with specified chapters. You may wish to have class members find in the filmstrip some principles which have been set forth in the textbook.

Chapters 1 and 2   *The Christian Teacher*
Chapter   3   *Selecting Aims*
Chapter   6   *Planning a Lesson*
Chapters 7 and 8   *Choosing Methods*
Chapter   9   *Testing Results*

The teaching situation used to illustrate chapter 6 will live more vividly if you use the film *Woman at the Well* (15 min. Sound).

There is a wealth of slides on the life of Christ. Some of these may be used as spot illustrations of situations to which the author refers. The teacher of this textbook should make a list of the slides available in the church library and, from the context, determine the points at which to throw selected slides on the screen as the material in the book is being presented.

For additional information and current prices see *Focus*, the audio-visual aids catalogue from your Baptist Book Store.

Church Study Course for Teaching and Training

THE CHURCH STUDY COURSE FOR TEACHING AND TRAINING began October 1, 1959. It is a merger of three courses previously promoted by the Sunday School Board—The Sunday School Training Course, the Graded Training Union Study Course, and the Church Music Training Course.

The course is fully graded. The system of awards provides a series of five diplomas of twenty books each for Adults or Young People, one diploma of ten books for Young People, two diplomas of five books each for Intermediates, and two diplomas of five books each for Juniors. Book awards earned previously in the Sunday School Training Course, the Graded Training Union Study Course, and the Church Music Training Course may be transferred to the new course.

The course is comprehensive, with books grouped into nineteen categories. The purpose of the course is to (1) help Christians to grow in knowledge and conviction; (2) help them grow toward maturity in Christian character and competence for service; (3) encourage them to participate worthily as workers in their churches; and (4) develop leaders for all phases of church life and work.

The church Study Course for Teaching and Training is promoted by the Baptist Sunday School Board, 127 Ninth Avenue, North, Nashville, Tennessee, through its Sunday School, Training Union, Church Music, and Church Administration departments, and by these same departments in the states affiliated with the Southern Baptist Convention. A complete description of the course and the system of awards may be found in the Church Study Course for Teaching and Training catalog, which may be obtained without charge from any one of these departments.

A record of all awards earned should be maintained in each church. A person should be designated by the Church to keep the files. Forms for such records may be ordered from any Baptist Book Store.

Requirements for Credit in Class or Home Study

IF CREDIT IS DESIRED for the study of this book in a class or by home study, the following requirements must be met:

I. IN CLASSWORK

1. The class must meet a minimum of seven and one-half clock hours. The required time does not include assembly periods. Ten class periods of forty-five minutes each are recommended. (If laboratory or clinical work is desired in specialized or technical courses, this requirement may be met by six clock hours of classwork and three clock hours of supervised laboratory or clinical work.)

2. A class member who attends all class sessions and completes the reading of the book within a week following the last class session will not be required to do any written work.

3. A class member who is absent from one or more class sessions must answer the questions (pp. 133–134) on all chapters he misses. In such a case, he must turn in his paper within a week, and he must certify that he has read the book.

4. The teacher should request an award for himself. A person who teaches a book in section B, C, or D of any category or conducts an approved unit of instruction for Nursery, Beginner, or Primary children will be granted an award in category 11, Special Studies, which will count as an elective on his own diploma. He should specify in his request the name of the book taught, or the unit conducted for Nursery, Beginner, or Primary children.

5. The teacher should complete the "Request for Book Awards—Class Study" (Form 150) and forward it within two weeks after the completion of the class to the Church Study Course Awards Office, 127 Ninth Avenue, North, Nashville 3, Tennessee.

II. IN HOME STUDY

1. A person who does not attend any class session may receive credit by answering all questions for written work as indicated in the book (pp. 133–134). When a person turns in his paper on home study, he must certify that he has read the book.

2. Students may find profit in studying the text together, but individual papers are required. Carbon copies or duplicates in any form cannot be accepted.

3. Home study work papers may be graded by the pastor or a person designated by him, or they may be sent to the Church Study Course Awards Office for grading. The form entitled "Request for Book Awards—Home Study" (Form 151) must be used in requesting awards. It should be mailed to Church Study Course Awards Office, 127 Ninth Avenue, North, Nashville 3, Tennessee.

III. CREDIT FOR THIS BOOK

This book is number 1741 in category 17, section A.

CHAPTER I

His Fitness for Teaching

NEVER was any one better fitted for his task than Jesus was for teaching. In qualifications as in other respects he was the ideal teacher. This is true whether viewed from the divine or the human angle. In the fullest sense he was "a teacher come from God." Many elements entered into this many-sided preparation. Some were human and others, divine. Some were inherent and others, developed. A consideration of them should stimulate us.

I. EMBODIED THE TRUTH

The most important element in the qualification of any teacher is what he is himself. One example is worth a hundred exhortations. "What you are thunders so loud I cannot hear what you say." The best binding for the Gospels is not Morocco, but human skin. It was this fact that led President Garfield to say that his ideal of a university was a log with Mark Hopkins on one end and a student on the other; Emerson to remark that the important thing is not what you learn but with whom you learn; and the noted superintendent, Stephen Tyng, to reply in answer to a request for his Sunday school constitution, "I am sorry but I cannot come."

"Truth incarnate is the only spiritual truth that makes an effective appeal. Hence every teacher must feel, 'My most effective lesson is myself.'"[1] This is so because truth is caught more than taught. Unconscious influ-

---

[1] McKinney, A. H., *The Sunday School Teacher at His Best,* p. 20, Fleming H. Revell Co., New York, 1915.
NOTE: Most of the works cited in this textbook are now out of print. Your church library may have copies.

1

ence is more effective than conscious. "The teacher's words will go only so far as the projectile power of a good life will send them." [1] It is the heft of the ax that gives it cutting power. Therefore the Sunday school teacher must be something as well as say something. "The teacher's life is the life of his teaching." It was what they were that did most to make great teachers of Arnold of Rugby, Phelps of Yale, Broadus of Southern Seminary, and Carroll of Southwestern.

Jesus was the living embodiment of truth. He said: "I am . . . the truth" (John 14: 6). He was 100 per cent what he taught. Whatever the subject, he incarnated it and taught from the overflow of his own life. S. D. Gordon has said: "Jesus was before he did, he lived what he taught, and lived it before he taught it, and lived it far more than he could teach it." [2] C. S. Beardslee puts it this way: "His ample soul gave ample room for the Holy Spirit's full anointing. . . . As you face his eye, you are facing fulness of light. . . . He had unlimited reserves of verity, majesty, beneficence, zeal, patience, persistence, and long suffering. . . . He showed dependents how to trust, subjects how to serve, rulers how to rule, neighbors how to be friends, the needy how to pray, the suffering how to bear, and all men how to die. . . . He is the teaching model for all time." [3]

This incarnation of truth grew out of two things. One was that he was God and possessed in perfection the qualities of God. He was the only perfect being. He differed from us in kind as well as in degree. Hence we can never approach his perfection. Also his embodiment of the truth grew out of the fact that he studied and experienced it, and made it a part of himself. "Jesus

[1] Quoted by Tidwell, J. B., in *The Sunday School Teacher Magnified,* p. 17, Fleming H. Revell Co., New York, 1918.
[2] *Quiet Talks on Home Ideals,* p. 114, Fleming H. Revell Co., New York, 1909.
[3] *Teacher Training with the Master Teacher,* pp. 162 ff, The Sunday School Times Co., Philadelphia, 1903.

increased in wisdom" (Luke 2: 52). He learned as a son
and brother in the home, through study and association
in the synagogue, and through life experiences. He suf-
fered temptation from the standpoint of self-preservation, social recognition, and the drive for power. The
writer of Hebrews says: "It was fitting that he [God]
. . . should make the pioneer of their salvation perfect
through suffering" (Heb. 2: 10).

The Master's embodiment of the truth affected his
teaching in at least two ways. In the first place it gave
a note of authority not found in that of the scribes and
rabbis—the official teachers of the times. Their knowledge was mainly from without, a matter of hearsay, and
they taught largely by quoting from authorities. His
was from within and needed not to be supported. "This
teacher was different. He quoted nobody; his own word
was offered as sufficient." [1] Therefore, he taught with
clarity, conviction, and power. The people were "astonished at his teaching, for he taught them as one who
had authority, and not as the scribes" (Mark 1: 22). His
living what he taught also inspired confidence in his
statements. People saw embodied in his practice what
he sought to get them to do. They observed how he experienced sorrow, criticism, disappointment, persecution.
His living reinforced and gave weight to what he said.
"The greatest thing the disciples got from his teaching
was not a doctrine but an influence. To the last hour
of their lives the big thing was that they had been with
him." [2] Therefore, "he appointed twelve, to be with him"
(Mark 3: 14).

As human teachers we can demonstrate in our lives the
"out-living of the indwelling Christ." Only thus can we
meet this first test of fitness.

[1] Barton, Bruce, *The Man Nobody Knows,* p. 22, The Bobbs-Merrill
Co., New York, 1925.
[2] Marquis, John A., *Learning to Teach from the Master Teacher,*
p. 68, The Westminster Press, Philadelphia, 1918.

II. DESIRED TO SERVE

One of the most essential elements in the qualifications of a teacher is an interest in people and a desire to help. Without that, one is but a "sounding brass or a tinkling cymbal," however well he knows the Bible, the pupil, and methods. Nothing can atone for a lack of interest in the welfare of persons. To be concerned about a large class, a perfect record, or teaching methods is not an adequate substitute for a concern for people.

On the other hand, a love for and desire to serve one's pupils will go a long way toward making up for deficiency in knowledge and teaching technique. Some of the most unlikely personalities the writer has known have been the most effective workers with Intermediates (the most critical age), and the explanation was that they genuinely loved that age group. Sooner or later, pupils realize this interest and respond to it. Everybody loves a lover.

Outstanding in the character of Jesus was his interest in the welfare of people. He was not as much concerned about creeds, ceremonials, organizations, or equipment as he was about persons. He saw them "like sheep without a shepherd" (Mark 6: 34). If Will Rogers could say that he never saw anyone he did not like, how much more could that be said of Jesus! When the Pharisees criticized his disciples for plucking grain on the sabbath, he defended them by saying: "The sabbath was made for man, not man for the sabbath" (Mark 2: 27). When the self-centered young miser stopped him by the roadside to inquire the way of life, it is said, "Jesus looking upon him loved him." (Mark 10: 21). When a man afflicted with the terrible disease of leprosy appealed to him he was so moved with sympathy that he "stretched out his hand and touched him" (Mark 1: 41). His heart went out to the critical scribes and jealous Pharisees, to the hated publicans and scorned sinners, to the blind, the deaf, and the lame.

He loved people and was interested in their problems. "He embodied and unburdened all the love of God; and he had compassion on all the ills of men." [1] The Master was not only concerned about people's problems but wanted to do something about them. He had a genuine missionary spirit and said that he came not to be served but to serve (Matt. 20: 28). He was not too tired to talk to a depraved woman at a well about the Water of life. He was not too proud to make a visit to the home of a despised tax collector. He braved the criticism of the religious leaders to associate with the sinful. The parables of the lost coin, lost sheep, and lost boy show his concern. His heart went out in sympathy to a needy world and his hand followed in helpful service.

This attitude has characterized every great teacher through the ages—Pantaenus as he started the first Christian school at Alexandria alongside a pagan university; Benedict as he organized a teaching order at Monte Cassino that influenced Europe for three centuries; Gerard Groote as he founded the Brothers of the Common Life to teach poor children; Loyola as he constituted the Jesuit order to teach youth; and Robert Raikes as he started the Sunday school movement which has gone around the world. The service motive is indispensable to successful teaching.

III. Believed in Teaching

Jesus saw in teaching the supreme opportunity for shaping the ideals, attitudes, and conduct of people. He was not primarily an orator, reformer, or ruler, but rather a teacher. To be sure he did not belong to the professional class of scribes and rabbis who gave minute

---

[1] Beardslee, C. S., *Teacher Training with the Master Teacher*, p. 47, The Sunday School Times Co., Philadelphia, 1903.

interpretations of the law, but he taught. He was in no
sense a "rabble rouser." He did not trust his cause to
mass meeting appeals, ritualistic procedure, or political
maneuvering, but rather to the long-drawn-out processes
of teaching and training. L. A. Weigle says: "Jesus
used the educational method rather than the method of
power politics, or propaganda or force." [1] And J. A.
Marquis adds: "Teaching was his chief business. He
was often a healer, sometimes a worker of miracles, frequently a preacher, but always a teacher. He did not
teach when he was not doing something else, but when
he was not teaching he was doing something else. He
made teaching the chief agency of redemption." [2]

Jesus' emphasis on teaching is evidenced by the fact
that he was generally recognized as a teacher. "As he
appears in the Gospels, he was thought of by his disciples and by his contemporaries as a teacher." [3] He was
called Teacher, Master, or Rabbi; all of which carry the
same general idea as when Nicodemus said: "Rabbi, we
know that you are a teacher come from God" (John 3:
2). At least forty-five times in the Four Gospels he was
called teacher, but never preacher. L. J. Sherrill says that
by including all of the terms equivalent to teacher we
have a total of sixty-one.[4] Norman Richardson points out
that "Master" is used sixty-six times in the King James
Version, fifty-four of which are from the Greek word
meaning teacher or schoolmaster.[5] Forty-five times he
was referred to as teaching and eleven times as preaching,

[1] *Jesus and the Educational Method,* p. 19, The Abingdon Press,
New York, 1939.
[2] *Learning to Teach from the Master Teacher,* pp. 76, 77, The
Westminster Press, Philadelphia, 1913.
[3] Bower, W. C., *Christ and Christian Education,* p. 18, Abingdon-
Cokesbury Press, Nashville, 1943.
[4] *The Rise of Christian Education,* p. 86, The Macmillan Co., New
York, 1944.
[5] *The Christ of the Classroom,* p. 11, The Macmillan Co., New York,
1931.

often coupled with teaching, as when he is spoken of as "teaching in their synagogues and preaching the gospel of the kingdom" (Matt. 4: 23). Not only the twelve, but also other disciples, and even his enemies, called him teacher.[1]

Likewise he called himself teacher, saying: "You call me Teacher and Lord; and you are right, for so I am" (John 13: 13). Also he called himself "light" which carries the idea of instruction. In this connection it is interesting to note that John the Baptist was always called preacher rather than teacher.[2]

Another indication of his stress on teaching is the terminology used to describe his followers and his message. They were not called subjects, retainers, or comrades. The expression "Christian" is used only three times in the New Testament to characterize them, and one of these in derision. Over against this is the fact that the term "disciple," which means "pupil" or "learner," is used 243 times to describe his followers. And his message is spoken of as "teaching" (thirty-nine times) and as "wisdom" (six times) rather than as address or sermon. The term "Sermon on the Mount" is not used by the New Testament writers but instead Matthew says: "He opened his mouth and taught them" (Matt. 5: 2). So it should be called the "Teaching on the Mount."

Also the Master's emphasis on teaching is indicated by the enthusiastic and aggressive way in which he carried on a teaching activity. He taught everywhere and at all times—in the Temple, in the synagogues, in the mountain, by the seaside, by the road, by a well, in the homes, at social gatherings, and in private. "He grudged even to healing, the hours in which he had opportunity

---

[1] See Williams, C. B., *The Function of Teaching in Christianity*, Chap. 1, Baptist Sunday School Board, Nashville, 1912.

[2] Trumbull, H. C., *Yale Lectures on the Sunday School*, p. 33, John D. Wattles, Philadelphia, 1893.

to declare his message."[1] Matthew says: "He went all
over Galilee, teaching in their synagogues and proclaiming the good news of the kingdom, and curing any disease
or sickness among the people" (Matt. 4: 23, Goodspeed's
translation). His work carried a didactic atmosphere
rather than that of impassioned address, for people felt
free to ask him questions, and he in turn asked them
questions.

He trained a group of teachers to carry on his work.
"During the closing days of his life work, he devoted
himself to teaching the small group of disciples who
gathered about him."[2] And he commanded these disciples to go to the ends of the earth, make disciples
(enlist in the school of Christ), baptize them (a teaching ordinance), and then teach them all the things he had
commanded (Matt. 28: 19-20). Jesus thoroughly believed in teaching, an indispensable prerequisite for any
teacher. He gave himself to it and forever dignified the
calling. "The supreme glory of the teaching profession
consists in the fact that when Jesus Christ faced his life
work—he chose to be a teacher."[3] George H. Palmer had
this spirit when he said: "So much do I believe in teaching that if I were able to do so I would pay for the
privilege rather than be paid for it."

IV. KNEW THE SCRIPTURES

Another essential for a teacher is to know the Bible, for
that is the primary material he is to use. Jesus was
thoroughly qualified in this respect. This was evidenced
in the temptation when he met each of the devil's efforts
to trap him by quoting the Scriptures (Matt. 4: 1-11). It
is seen in the conversation that took place on the walk

[1] Curtis, W. A., *Jesus Christ the Teacher*, p. 12, Oxford University Press, 1943.
[2] Kent, Charles F., *Great Teachers of Judaism and Christianity*, p. 108, Eaton and Mains, New York, 1911.
[3] Richardson, N. E., *The Christ of the Classroom*, p. 93, The Macmillan Co., New York, 1931.

to Emmaus when he explained the teachings in the Scriptures relative to himself (Luke 24: 27). During his ministry he quoted from at least twenty of the books of the Old Testament and showed thorough familiarity with its contents. In fact his grasp of it was such that he contrasted its inadequacy with the fulness of his own teaching (Matt. 5: 17-48). He not only knew the Scriptures but had assimilated them to such an extent that he could apply them freely to the issues of the day.

This mastery came not only because of his deity but also because of his study. The beginning was in infancy in the Jewish home whose very atmosphere was religious and educational. B. A. Hinsdale says: "The very household duties the mother performed molded her children in accordance with national discipline."[1]

And Harold Wilson states: "Even as he [the Jewish child] lay in her arms, his eyes would be drawn to many objects, the religious meaning of which his mother would explain to him."[2] Among them were the kissing of the fingers which handled the Scripture parchments kept over the door or strapped to the wrist or forehead; the sight of the colored fringes of his father's outer garment reminding of the commandments of the Lord; the daily prayers and thanksgiving, especially at meals, the weekly observance, particularly the lighting of the sabbath fire and lamp; the annual ceremonials, such as the feasts of Passover and Tabernacles; and the solemn presentation to God of the firstborn male of flock and herd. So in the home Jesus learned the Scriptures and grew in wisdom as well as stature. "Nazareth is the double underscoring in red under every sentence he spoke."

Also he learned in the synagogue, which was practically universal in his time and attendance customary

[1] *Jesus as a Teacher,* p. 28, The Christian Publishing Co., St. Louis, 1895.
[2] *Jesus at School,* p. 51, The National Sunday School Union, London.

if not compulsory. Luke says: "He went to the synagogue, as his custom was, on the sabbath day" (Luke 4:
16). Wilson thinks Jesus attended at least once each
sabbath for twenty years or more.[1] Services were held
on the sabbath, Monday, and Thursday, and feast and
fast days. They were definitely instructional. The Law
(first five books of the Bible) was read by a reader, explained a verse at a time by an interpreter, and applied
to the lives of the people. So it was covered in three to
three and a half years somewhat as our Uniform Lessons. The second lesson of the day was taken from the
prophets and read and explained three verses at a time.
It was that which Jesus read in the synagogue at Nazareth, as mentioned by Luke (4: 17-19). Sometimes questions were asked and answers given. In addition, certain
Scripture passages were recited in concert. Thus Jesus
learned the Law and the prophets and was able to con-
fute the rabbis with the question: "Have ye not read?"

Connected with the synagogue was also an elementary
school for boys, meeting each week day. It was required
wherever there were as many as twenty-five pupils, and
attendance was compulsory. In fact no orthodox Jew
was supposed to live in a town without one, nor on the
opposite side of a stream from one unless the stream was
safely bridged. The boy started at about six, and until
ten studied the Scriptures beginning with Leviticus. He
covered the Law, history, prophets, and poetry, thus getting the religious, moral, and ceremonial teachings. From
the tenth to about the fifteenth year he studied the oral
interpretations of the Law, and at thirteen he became a
"son of the Law" and a responsible member of the synagogue congregation. "That he must almost have known
the Sacred Scriptures by heart is clear," says Canon
Farrar, "not only from his direct quotations, but also

---

[1] *Jesus at School,* p. 89, The National Sunday School Union,
London.

from the numerous allusions which he made to the Law, and to Isaiah, Jeremiah, Daniel, Joel, Hosea, Micah, Zechariah, Malachi, and above all to the book of Psalms." [1] Jesus was able to hold his own not only with the learned rabbis in the Temple at the age of twelve, but with his severest critics at all times.

V. Understood Human Nature

Along with knowing the Scriptures it is important to understand human nature. In fact in many ways it is a more important qualification. For one is not able to apply the Bible to life until he understands the pupil and his needs. Anyone who deals with human nature must know something about it. Just as the physician must be able to diagnose his patient before knowing what medicine to prescribe, so the teacher must understand human life and its problems before applying the scriptural remedy. In the last analysis we are not teaching the Bible but persons. Even the Scriptures themselves were given for teaching, correction, and discipline "that the man of God may be complete" (2 Tim. 3: 17). It is exceedingly important, then, to understand the persons with whom we deal.

Jesus not only understood the Jewish mind in general as to factions and sects, but he was also a master in penetrating the heart and understanding the inner workings of the individual mind. The Bible says: "He himself knew what was in man" (John 2: 25). Moffatt translates it, "Well did he know what was in human nature." How much that sentence carries perhaps no one will ever be able to know. Undoubtedly the Master plumbed human life to its very depths. Certainly he was able to tell whether his hearers were good or bad, attentive or inattentive, friendly or unfriendly, interested in

[1] Quoted by Hinsdale, B. A., in *Jesus as a Teacher*, p. 38, The Christian Publishing Co., St. Louis, 1895.

his instruction or uninterested, understanding his teaching or confused by it, agreeing with what he taught or critical of it. Had he not had this knowledge, he would not only have been unable to teach as effectively as he did, but also he would have been caught often in the traps his designing enemies set for him. With this knowledge he was able to know his learner's abilities, needs, attitudes, and motives and to teach in the light of them. "From a pedagogical standpoint, his intuition was the first condition of his marvelous power as a teacher." [1]

At least a half dozen instances evidence his keen insight into human nature—even the very thoughts of people. While the scribes thought within themselves that he blasphemed when he told the palsied man his sins were forgiven, "Jesus, knowing their thoughts, said, 'Why do you think evil in your hearts?'" (Matt. 9: 4). When the disciples complained at his saying that they must eat of his flesh and drink of his blood in order to have life, "Jesus, knowing in himself that his disciples murmured at it, said to them . . . , 'There are some of you that do not believe.' For Jesus knew from the first who those were that did not believe, and who it was that should betray him" (John 6: 61, 64).

When the Pharisees and Herodians sought to trap him, "knowing their hypocrisy, he said to them, 'Why put me to the test?' (Mark 12: 15). When he saw Nathaniel he said: "Behold, an Israelite indeed, in whom is no guile!" (John 1: 47). When the Samaritan woman was asked to call her husband and said that she had none, he answered, "You are right in saying, 'I have no husband'; for you have had five husbands, and he whom you now have is not your husband" (John 4: 17-18). He knew people and taught to meet their deep-down hidden needs, of which they themselves were often unaware.

[1] Hinsdale, B. A., *Jesus as a Teacher,* p. 50, The Christian Publishing Company, St. Louis, 1895.

VI. Mastered the Art

It is not here asserted that Jesus consciously and purposely studied teaching methods and procedures, and sought deliberately to follow them. Possibly he did. Probably he did not. But it still remains that he had such a grasp of teaching as to be thoroughly at home at the task. Intuitively or through assimilation he was a master of teaching methods. He set forth no particular psychological principle, educational theory, or pedagogical practice; yet he grasped the essential elements in all of these and used them effectively. He used methods with perfect freedom and efficiency. Apparently they came to him naturally. Out of the fulness of his resources he met each teaching situation as it arose and used the procedure needed. He was so far ahead of others that W. A. Squires very appropriately gave his book the title *The Pedagogy of Jesus in the Twilight of Today*.[1] The best modern teachers have not caught up with him. We shall ever be learning from him.

That he was a master of the teaching art is shown by the fact that he used from time to time, at least in embryo, practically every method in use today—questions, lectures, stories, conversations, discussions, dramatics, objects, projects, and demonstrations. These we shall study more in detail later on. His mastery of the teaching art is also evidenced by the procedure that he followed; for when broken up into their component parts, his teaching activities are found to have the proper beginning, development, and conclusion. To this also we shall give attention later. His approach was direct, his illustrations to the point, and his application well made. He was master of the art of teaching.

In this mastery of the teaching art we shall do well

---

[1] George H. Doran Co., New York, 1927.

to follow his example. Consecration, fervor, and faith-
fulness will not make up for a lack of knowledge of
teaching methods, nor will they atone for weakness in
procedure. As a rule, teachers are not born, but made.
At least, as has been said, they are "not born made."
Careful study and painstaking practice are necessary. It
is hoped that this book will contribute some to that end.
Other books on teaching should be studied and mastered,
as well as books on pupils and their needs. Everything
else being equal, God can use a trained teacher much
better than an untrained one. We owe it to ourselves
and our pupils to be the best teachers we possibly
can.

In the light of Jesus' perfect personality, spirit of service, confidence in teaching, knowledge of the Scriptures
and humanity, and grasp of teaching methods and processes, he was the best qualified teacher the world has
ever known. He was indeed the "Master Teacher" as
Horne has characterized him in the title of his book. Or
as J. L. Corzine has well said: "Jesus is more than Master Teacher. He is the 'Peerless Teacher.'"[1] "A way-
side rock or a stool borrowed from a cottage, when he
sat down upon it, became a seat of worldwide authority
which sovereigns and pontiffs might envy."[2] He is our
incomparable model, and we shall ever be learning from
his methods as well as his messages. As Martha has said:
"The Teacher is here" (John 11: 28). "Unlike the religious teachers of his time, Jesus taught with an authority
of his own. He did not proceed as did the scribes by re-
hearsing the sayings of others. He spoke from the conscious passion of truth in himself."[3]

[1] "Jesus More than Master Teacher," article in *Seminar on
Religious Education*, p. 51, edited by W. Perry Crouch, Unpublished
paper.
[2] Curtis, W. A., *Jesus Christ the Teacher*, p. 16, Oxford University
Press, 1943.
[3] Stevens, G. B., *The Teaching of Jesus*, p. 35, The Macmillan Co.,
New York, 1902.

TEACHING AIDS

BLACKBOARD OUTLINE

I. Embodied the truth
II. Desired to serve
III. Believed in teaching
IV. Knew the Scriptures
V. Understood human nature
VI. Mastered the art

TOPICS FOR DISCUSSION

1. Why is it so important to live what one teaches?
2. What is the value of wanting to serve?
3. Why was Jesus so committed to teaching?
4. What present-day agency is the synagogue elementary school most like?
5. Why is it so important to understand the pupil?
6. How did Jesus learn how to teach?

CHAPTER II

Characteristics of His Pupils

IF ONE HAS the idea that those whom Jesus taught, even the twelve, were ideal persons, he is in for disillusionment. Since they are Bible characters, and we are so far removed from them, we are likely to idealize them. But they were very much human with the imperfections and frailties of human beings. For humanity was then very largely as it is now. Though environmental conditions change, human nature remains essentially the same.

This is true of all ages, climes, and conditions of culture. Will Rogers voiced the idea well when he said, regarding the accomplishments of a peace conference in Europe, "There is just one little matter yet to be worked out, and that is the problem of human nature." So it is always. A look at those Jesus taught will be both informing and suggestive, if not encouraging, to us as teachers. There was an inner circle, a larger group of followers, and an outer circle of critics and indifferent.

I. UNDEVELOPED

These persons with whom Jesus dealt were far from perfect when he began with them. And when he completed his work, too, for that matter. They were ideal characters merely in embryo. They were saints only in the making. They fulfilled well one of George A. Coe's threefold requirements for a teaching situation, that of "immature beings." A long way had to be traveled and much patience exercised before they would become full-grown Christians. Many disappointments and discouragements would come along the way. Only one with insight into the future, infinite love and patience, and enduring energy and persistence could have taken this group and done what the Master did with them.

One does not have to look very deep to see how undeveloped and imperfect they were. John, who was to become the beloved disciple, had a temper not yet brought under control, and he failed utterly to show the mature love for the uncharitable Samaritans which Jesus sought to have his disciples manifest. Simon who was to be given the name Peter (stone) lacked a lot of having that solid disposition the name suggests when he promised Jesus to stay with him even if all others deserted, and then in a few hours not only denied three times that he ever knew him but actually punctuated his denial with unseemly language.

Thomas was so hardheaded about believing that Christ had risen from the dead that it took special effort on the Teacher's part to demonstrate the fact to his satisfaction. Judas after close association with, and teaching by, the Master was never developed to the point of being able to resist the temptation to betray him for financial gain. All of them were suffering either from the disease of arrested development or that of progressive perversity.

To take this small group of undeveloped, unlikely individuals and grow them into a band of developed, well-rounded persons who have been an inspiration to the world is a marvel of the teaching and training art. It has never been surpassed by any other teacher throughout the ages, and has been an inspiration and encouragement to Christian teachers ever since. No one knows what possibilities are wrapped up in a seemingly unlikely boy or girl, or what may be done with him. Little did the old teacher of the Brethren of the Common Life realize as he took off his hat in the presence of his pupils, saying that he never knew when he might be in the

presence of one greater than the emperor, that one of his
pupils, Martin Luther, would turn out to be just that!

It is our privilege through teaching to change lives that
are immature and seemingly of little worth, and to develop them into outstanding characters. A crippled
blacksmith gathered from the streets a group of four
unlikely young boys and patiently taught them. He lived
to see them grow into a foreign missionary, a member of
a President's cabinet, a private secretary to a President,
and a President of the United States, Warren G. Harding!

II. IMPULSIVE

Jesus' pupils were more than undeveloped. They were
developed in the wrong way. Some of them were very
much given to impetuousness. Peter was especially so.
In fact he is the champion example. "He was a man of
impulse, a rushing, impetuous type of man, like a mountain stream hurrying over the rocks on its way to the
valley below. His reactions came in spurts. He moved
first and thought it over later." [1] A striking instance was
his jumping into the sea on a cool spring morning and
swimming to Jesus on the shore when he might have
gone ashore by boat (John 21: 7). Another was his request to have even his hands and face bathed when he
had held back from foot washing until told he had no
part with Christ unless he submitted (John 13: 9). A
more striking instance was his sudden slashing off of
the ear of the high priest's servant when they had come
to arrest his Lord (John 18: 10).

John was likewise impetuous. Jesus himself termed
him a "son of thunder." Says Charles R. Brown: "He
was a child of the storm. There were times when he
was hot and terrible in his outbursts of feeling. He could
upon occasion show himself a whirlwind of enthusiasm

---

[1] Brown, Charles R., *These Twelve*, p. 4, The Century Co., New
York, 1926.

or a tornado of wrath. So far from being a placid, passive milk-and-water sort of man, he was a man of violent temper."[1] This was particularly manifested when he and other disciples entered a Samaritan village to arrange entertainment for Jesus and were refused because he was headed toward Jerusalem, and the Samaritans would have nothing to do with Jews if they could avoid it. John was so mad that he said: "Lord, do you want us to bid fire come down from heaven and consume them?" (Luke 9: 54). It was a long jump from that attitude to the one of a gentle old man saying: "He who does not love does not know God" (1 John 4: 8).

Others of the inner circle and of those not so close in were likewise rather impulsive. Simon the Zealot, as the title indicates, belonged to a rather radical political party. As Brown says: "He may be either an asset or a liability. He is steam in the boiler, but that steam may drive an unpiloted ship upon the rocks, or, escaping by some mischance, it may scald the passengers to death."[2] Whether radical personally or not, he at least belonged to a rather revolutionary group when Jesus selected him as a follower.

John the Baptist also had a thunderous disposition. We think of him as anything but a conservative as in plain garb he came from his fasts to go up and down the land preaching the gospel of repentance to a perverse and wicked generation. "He emerged with flaming eyeballs to deliver his uncompromising challenge. His fiery language burned through to consciences that were overgrown with a very thick crust."[3] He had the reformer's temperament. Even Matthew was not too conservative. Says T. R. Glover: "The publican in the group is of much the same type; he is ready to leave his busi-

[1] *These Twelve*, p. 49, The Century Co., New York, 1926.
[2] *These Twelve*, p. 167, The Century Co., New York, 1926.
[3] Barton, Bruce, *The Man Nobody Knows*, p. 67, The Bobbs-Merrill Co., Indianapolis, 1925.

ness and his custom house at a word—once more the
impulsive nature and the warm heart." [1]

Such was the impetuousness of these disciples and
others that Jesus was constantly urging them to count
the cost before they acted. So outstanding were these
traits that if one were recommending some of them for
the pastorate of a prominent church today, he would
probably feel it necessary to put in a qualifying clause
regarding these characteristics. But let it be remembered
that then as well as now not the staid, intellectual, conservative persons, but the aggressive, venturesome, daring
ones have been those who have carried forward most
effectively the work of the kingdom of God. The pupil
whom you feel most constrained to hold back, and even
"sit on," may be the one through whom you will have
your best chance at fame. We may thank God for men
of impulse if they are rightly guided.

III. SINFUL

The Master not only confronted personalities with
undeveloped characters and impulsive dispositions, but
also with definite tendencies toward sin. While some of
them came to be outstanding Christians, they were not
always as angelic as our imagination or the artists may
have painted them. There were urges and drives in them
that, uncontrolled by Christian ideals, would inevitably
lead to positive evils. Actually such did happen and they
did things which later they probably wished might be
stricken from the records.

In fact some whom Jesus taught and whose lives were
changed by him were already far down the pathway of
evil. One, though he associated with Jesus for years, and
even became treasurer, finally yielded to greed and sold
his Master for thirty pieces of silver.

---

[1] *The Jesus of History,* p. 77, George H. Doran Co., New York, 1917.

But Judas was not the only one even of the inner circle whose sinful tendencies got the upper hand of him, at least temporarily. Peter could swear if it would help hide his identity and save him from a tight place. John not only gave vent to his temper and his prejudice, but also to his pride, and asked for the privilege of sitting at the right hand of Jesus. And James joined in this desire for social recognition and political power. "There is friction among them which is not unnatural in a group of men with ambitions. Even at the Last Supper their minds run on thrones"[1] (Mark 9: 33; 10: 37; Luke 22: 24). In fact the whole group argued about the matter of greatness.

Beyond the circle of the twelve was the money-loving, grasping, extortioner Zaccheus who as tax collector pressured all he could get out of needy people. Then there was Mary Magdalene with seven devils to her credit. Also, the fallen woman who washed his feet with her tears and dried them with her hair. And there was the free love woman whom he had taught by the well, who had five husbands on her string. Likewise there were the accusers of an adulteress who slipped away when Jesus asked that the one without sin cast the first stone. No, the Master's was not an ideal class that assembled under ideal conditions to be taught by the ideal teacher. Rather they were people with like passions as ourselves, which passions often got the upper hand of them. Pride, greed, and lust beset their lives and had to be met by Jesus' precepts and influence.

What was true then is also true now. One never knows what lies ahead for members of his class. Uncontrolled instincts inevitably lead to ruin. Beneath the fair exterior of a boy may be tendencies to crime that, unless checked, will land him in the penitentiary. Such has hap-

---

[1] Glover, T. R., *The Jesus of History*, p. 78, George H. Doran Co., New York, 1917.

pened over and over again. That cultured and refined
girl, wearing the very mark of innocence, may be harbor-
ing ideals or developing passions that will lead to a life
of shame. That also has happened all too frequently.
No teacher can know all the evil thoughts and purposes
in the minds of those in his class. It may be said of most
of us as John Bradford said of himself when he saw a
criminal pass by, "There but for the grace of God goes
John Bradford." We must teach always to curb sinful
tendencies and transform character into the likeness of
Jesus.

IV. PERPLEXED

Those whom Jesus taught were confronted by many
perplexing problems, and they brought them to him for
solution. Sometimes they were not sincere in the perplexities that they presented, and raised them more to
trap him than to find solutions for themselves. He readily discerned this fact but recognized them nevertheless,
and often turned the tables on the questioners. The
issues were of all kinds, and dealt with many phases of
life. In answering them Christ not only helped those
whom he taught personally, but also all others through
the ages. Since John indicates that the world would
hardly contain all of the books necessary to record the
complete teachings of Christ, it is likely that there were
many issues raised about which we do not know.

A number of very personal and intimate problems
were presented. These touched many phases of life in a
vital way. There was the request of a brother for his
part of an estate, a self-preservative desire. Along with
that was the matter of ambition and social recognition
raised by the disciples as they argued along the way as
to which one was the greatest. This was also a native
urge and desire. How he might secure eternal life was
the problem of the rich ruler, and apparently of Nico-

demus. Others faced questions as to the deity of Christ, tolerance of other workers, when and how to worship, the resurrection, the greatest of the Commandments, the problem of fasting, how demons were cast out and other difficult matters. Still other personal problems discussed were pride, anger, lust, worry, and coveteousness. In fact most of the personal issues faced today were confronted by those whom the Master taught.

There were likewise many questions of a social nature or involving relationships to others. Simon Peter wanted to know how many times to forgive a brother who had sinned against him. Should he stop at seven or go beyond? (Matt. 18: 21-35). The Pharisees sought to catch him with the query, "Is it lawful to divorce one's wife for any cause?" (Matt. 19: 3). Similarly the Sadducees, seeking to show the impossibility of the resurrection, raised the question as to which of seven husbands would be the woman's in the other world (Matt. 22: 23-33). A somewhat broader question was raised by the lawyer on the whole problem of neighborliness, when to justify his own selfishness he asked, "And who is my neighbor?" (Luke 10: 29).

Another problem, very ticklish in those days, was that of loyalty to government in the matter of tax paying, brought out when the scribes and chief priests asked if it were lawful to give tribute to Caesar (Luke 20: 22). And of course there was the sabbath question brought to the fore when the disciples plucked grain on that day as they went through the fields (Mark 2: 23-28). Jesus even imagined some, such as that of a sheep falling into the ditch and a king going to war. Other problems include giving, praying, service, criticism, and retaliation.

In the light of these many questions it would look as if Jesus spent much of his time in solving personal problems rather than in giving general instruction. And this he seems to have done. For life problems are always much the same and as he met those of the people then he threw light on ours today. Especially is this true since he dealt with fundamental principles more than specific remedies. Thus he was counselor as well as instructor, as we shall likely have to be if we render the most vital and valuable service to our pupils who face serious issues today. No one ever met problems and perplexities as well as he, or gave more helpful general principles for universal solution. He was a master in counseling as well as a master in teaching.

V. IGNORANT

To say that Jesus' pupils possessed darkened and dull intellects as well as perplexed souls seems almost like adding insult to injury. But such must be done if one is to get a complete picture of the situation Jesus confronted in his teaching. His disciples came from the common walks of life rather than from the professional classes, and consequently did not have the cultural background that the professional leaders did. This had its handicap. There were many things they were not prepared to understand as their minds were not able to grasp all truth.

But that was not the only difficulty. A materialistic conception of life and ritualistic idea of religion interfered since spiritual truths are spiritually discerned. Both ignorance and a wrong viewpoint handicap a teacher. Either an intellectual fog or a mental rut is hard to get out of. Jesus faced both in his teaching, as nearly every teacher does. And though he was a master in clarifying truth, it is a matter of record that either he was not understood or was misunderstood much of the time by the rank and file, the professional religious leaders, and even the inner circle. "He selected a small band with a view to training them to leadership, yet they could not understand, much less explain to others, the principles that were the corner stone of the faith they were to teach. . . . For the three years he taught them they were a continual disappointment to him." [1]

A very striking instance of this misunderstanding was his teaching on the nature of the kingdom. In spite of all that he said about its personal, inner, subjective nature, there was a general expectation that he would set up a kingdom based on power like earthly rulers. This was true even of the closest followers such as James and John who made a bid for places on his right and left hand—prime minister and secretary of state!

It is likewise evident that he was not understood on the subject of the resurrection, either his or ours. Though he had told them he would arise on the third day, no one seemed to expect it. In fact they were actually surprised at his rising. As we have seen, one of the disciples, Thomas, had to have special evidence to be convinced. Even the purpose of his death was not clear, for Paul speaks of the cross as a stumbling block to the Jews. And as important and seemingly simple a matter as the requirements for discipleship seems not to have been clear even to one as well trained as Nicodemus.

So in spite of the clarity of Jesus' thinking and the vividness of his expression, even the brightest and most interested of his pupils failed to grasp his meaning. It is probably not too much to say that throughout his entire ministry he was continually disappointed because of their inability to understand the truths taught. If that happened to him, we are not to be surprised if it happens to us. And since he did not allow himself to be discouraged by it, neither should we, but rather we should keep patiently on as he did. As Jesus said of Peter, so must we learn to say of each pupil, "Thou art . . . thou shalt be."

---

[1] Marquis, John A., *Learning to Teach from the Master Teacher*, p. 53, The Westminster Press, Philadelphia, 1913.

VI. PREJUDICED

It would seem to be enough for even the Master Teacher to have had to face pupils that were immature, sinful, distraught, and dull, without having any other difficulty to meet. But one cannot stop there, for the picture is not yet complete. Their mental attitudes were anything but favorable to the truths being presented by Jesus. At least that was true of many of them, or of most of them regarding some things.

John was so biased as to be unwilling for any one not of his group to cast out demons and do good (Mark 9: 38). In fact, prejudice was at the root of some of the problems previously mentioned. In the parable of the sower the first kind of soil described was the roadside—that hard, impenetrable kind into which seed could not easily enter (Matt. 13: 3-23). This is a fine picture of the prejudiced or close-minded attitude that would not even consider the truth being presented. And evidently Jesus was faced by that very kind of people when he gave the parable, since he taught to meet the needs of life as he confronted them. It is the sort of situation confronted by every Sunday school teacher every time he teaches. For whether the lesson is on conversion, tithing, temperance, or any other topic, there will be background practices and prejudices that will keep pupils from participating with open minds. A completely unbiased attitude is hard to find. Intolerance is worse than ignorance.

When Jesus talked about the resurrection, he met the sneering attitude of the aristocratic, rationalistic Sadducees who in order to show its ridiculousness brought up the question of the future husband of the woman who had been seven times married. They were the intellectual high-brows and critics of their day. When he sought to show God's love for every creature, no matter how sinful, he faced the intellectual daggers of the self-righteous Pharisees who felt themselves too good to associate with the common man. So he had to coin the story of the prodigal son, or present the contrast of the Pharisee and publican engaged in prayer. When the rich young ruler knelt in his presence and humbly inquired the way of eternal life, it looked for once as if an open-minded inquirer had come. But when Jesus told him to sell all he had, give it to the poor, and follow him, the young man's expression changed and he "went away sorrowful for he had great possessions" (Mark 10: 22).

So he faced biased pupils. They were willing to have their stomachs filled and their diseases healed, but they did not want their interests crossed or their way of living changed. And the world is much like that today. People would like to be healed and freed from eternal punishment; but when it comes to repentance, service, and sacrifice, they lose interest and turn away. It is still a difficult task to convince a man against his will. Closed and prejudiced minds are about our greatest obstacles as teachers.

VII. UNSTABLE

If Jesus' disciples had only been able to carry out faithfully that which they understood and received with open minds, it would not have been so bad. But they did not even do this. Human perversity is such that the will, as well as the intellect and the affections, is depraved. This was true of his disciples as well as others of his day. Many were unable to give up other interests and face the hardships and discouragements necessary to carry on with him. Interest waned and even his best friends hesitated to go on. His picture of thin soil and a quick growth, soon withered by the scorching sun, is a good description of the situation he faced.

Then as now temptation, tribulation, and persecution soon thinned the ranks. Says Marquis, "A good many people started to follow the Master, but after a while lost zest and dropped out. Even he could not hold them. After three years of the best teaching the world ever heard, during which he spoke to thousands of people, one hundred and twenty were left, and most of them had to be bolstered up by his post-resurrection ministry." [1] What a picture of the result of the lifework of the world's greatest Teacher! Even off-brand cults seem to surpass that today.

A striking instance of weakness is the case of the rich young ruler, previously referred to, who, though intelligent and interested, was not able to give up his possessions even for Christ. Never did any young man forfeit such an opportunity for fellowship, service, and fame. Another case already mentioned is that of Peter who, after all of his promises of staying faithful to the end, though all others deserted, turned his back on his Master and denied him with an oath when he faced an unfriendly crowd.

At one time during Christ's ministry the falling away became so general that he turned rather pathetically to the faithful few who remained and said: "Will you also go away?" (John 6: 67). And after his crucifixion we know that even his most loyal followers went back to their old jobs evidently feeling that the cause was lost. "Those Eleven Men ran like frightened sheep, crawled off into the shadows to hide from the pointing fingers of Jerusalem." [2]

If all of these things happened to Jesus who was so far beyond anything we can hope to be, and his work for the time turned out with such seemingly disappointing

[1] *Learning to Teach from the Master Teacher,* p. 57, The Westminster Press, Philadelphia, 1913.
[2] Mead, Frank S., *The March of Eleven Men,* p. 21, Grosset and Dunlap, New York, 1931.

results, we ought not to be surprised when our work does
not turn out as we would like. When it is easier to get
a class than hold it, and when so many boys and girls fall
out in the Intermediate department, we need to remember
the Great Teacher and take courage.

If the reader feels that this chapter leaves the situation
at too low an ebb, let him remember that in spite of the
difficulties and discouragements Jesus faced, he worked
on patiently and made of this group the most effective
corps of disciples and teachers the cause ever had.
T. R. Glover says: "The greatest miracle in history
seems to be the transformation that Jesus effected in
those men." [1] Strengthened by his teaching, his resurrection and the Spirit, they went forth to transform the
world, ten of them giving even their very lives in carrying on the work. They started Christianity on its worldwide course. "Judged by results Jesus turned out the
greatest generation of teachers the world has ever known
—twelve men who afterwards turned the world upside
down." [2] How he made them into such stalwart characters we shall notice in further studies. What we have
sought here has been to see our pupils in the light of
those whom Jesus taught, understand more clearly our
tasks, and be encouraged to carry on faithfully.

[1] *The Jesus of History*, p. 85, George H. Doran Co., New York, 1917.
[2] Marquis, John A., *Learning to Teach from the Master Teacher*,
pp. 27, 49, The Sunday School Times Co., Philadelphia, 1913.

TEACHING AIDS

BLACKBOARD OUTLINE

I. Undeveloped
II. Impulsive
III. Sinful
IV. Perplexed
V. Ignorant
VI. Prejudiced
VII. Unstable

TOPICS FOR DISCUSSION

1. Classify the twelve apostles as to temperament.
2. Give other instances showing lack of development.
3. What are the psychological roots of sin?
4. Compare problems in Jesus' day and ours.
5. Why were Jesus' pupils unable to grasp his teaching?
6. Discuss the causes of prejudiced attitudes.
7. Give reasons for waning interest in his work.

CHAPTER III

His Aims in Instructing

ONE OF the most important helps in teaching is that of clear-cut and specific aims. Many teachers work from month to month without any definite purpose except to present the material given them. This accounts for much lifelessness and lack of interest. Without an objective one lacks definiteness, perspective, and purpose. Also he lacks the means of measuring the results of his teaching. He is headed nowhere and does not know whether or not he has arrived.

With Jesus, however, it was different. He never taught merely because he was called upon. He did it on purpose, and he always had definite ends to accomplish. He realized what he wanted and set out to attain it. He knew where he was going and moved steadily on, undaunted by opposition or failure. "I came that they may have life" (John 10: 10). He sought "to transform the lives of his disciples and through them to transform other lives and regenerate human society." [1] Many things are included in this general aim.

I. FORM RIGHT IDEALS

Ideals are the most powerful impersonal forces in the world for character building. They provide the chart, the guide for life's course. They control to a great extent our conduct. Instinctive urges are largely dominated by them. A young person will refuse to drink, smoke, or dance mainly because of ideals. A youth was led to

[1] Piper, D. R., *How Would Jesus Teach*, p. 34, David C. Cook Pub. Co., Elgin, 1931.

resist the temptation of his companions by the consciousness of the fact that none of his ancestry had been guilty of such a practice. W. S. Athearn was right when he said: "Ideals are the pulleys over which we lift original nature to higher levels." They determine the effectiveness of our emotional yearnings and deliberate resolutions.

The results of the pledges of three consecrated Christians to be stewards of God with their possessions may be entirely different though they are equally sincere. One may have the conception that he is to give when he feels like it and realizes no obligation unless the preacher moves him; another may believe in tithing—no more and no less, whatever his income; and the third may consider that all belongs to God and give as much as nine-tenths, if his income is large. Ideals determine the differences in the outcomes of their resolutions. Proper knowledge is necessary to proper living. One cannot live much better than he knows. Right conduct is rooted in right understanding. Whoever, therefore, fashions the ideals of people, determines in a large measure their destiny.

Very naturally, then, Jesus sought to form right ideals. "You, therefore, must be perfect, as your heavenly Father is perfect" (Matt. 5: 48). He sought particularly to give a clearer understanding of the nature of God and his attitude toward humanity.

He presents him as a loving Father disturbed about the sinfulness of man rather than as a heartless monarch unconcerned about needy people. The parables of the lost coin, lost sheep, and lost boy reveal the heart attitude of God. He presents man not as adequate in himself but as requiring the regenerating influence of God's Spirit if he is to enter the kingdom of God. This is clearly shown in the conversation with Nicodemus (John 3: 1-14). He outlined in the Teaching on the Mount, especially the

Beatitudes, the qualities and practices that should characterize a citizen of the kingdom in private living and in public relations. He warned people against pride, covetousness, being angry with one's brother, and looking lustfully on a woman. He gave a philosophy for the guidance of conduct, which after all is the most important thing in life, as W. J. McGlothlin decided when he heard a man following him in a park at night and was more concerned about the man's philosophy of life than whether he was a larger man, a Negro, or carried a gun.

The people flocked to Jesus because he fed them the truths their hungry hearts craved. Sunday school teachers may well learn a lesson from this fact. Our pupils will come to our classes if we feed them regularly. As the birds at a certain spot in central Europe returned systematically to that particular place because a man had made provision in his will for them to be fed there regularly, so our pupils will come back if we give them something worth while. All of the responsibility for building up a Sunday school class should not be on the visitors. The major part rests on the teaching which is enriched by visitation. There should be a pull from within through instruction as well as a push from without through persuasion. "No amount of fervor, no fund of anecdote, no fluency of speech can be made a substitute for imparting knowledge." [1]

In these days when emphasis is being given to problem solving and the life-situation approach in teaching, let us not forget the value of implanting divine truths in the minds of pupils and building life ideals. Major ideals or sentiments are necessary for unifying life, psychologists say. "As he thinketh in his heart, so is he" (Prov. 23: 7).

[1] Marquis, John A., *Learning to Teach from the Master Teacher*, p. 11, The Westminster Press, Philadelphia, 1913.

II. FIX STRONG CONVICTIONS

Jesus did not stop with imparting knowledge about spiritual and moral matters. He knew very well the inadequacy of information alone to overcome instinctive urges and evil environment. One may know ever so much about the evils of sex perversion, the harm of liquor, and the dangers in gambling, and still indulge in any or all of them. Men have been found in houses of ill fame with tracts on purity in their pockets. A tramp straggling on to a college campus read Greek as fluently as English until a crowd of students gathered, and then taking off his hat passed it around for a nickel or a dime that he might be able to buy more liquor.

It has been said that scarcely a major evil has been exposed but that some college graduate has been found to be prominently connected with it. More than five hundred college graduates have been rescued in the slums of New York City, some of whom had gone there to do uplift work. No, the Master was not deluded into the belief that knowledge alone is a cure-all. When he said, "The truth will make you free" (John 8: 32), he said it to those Jews who believed on him, and he conditioned it on their abiding in his word.

So the Teacher sought to deepen conviction as well as to implant truth. In other words he recognized the necessity of arousing feeling and developing attitudes. His ultimate aim was the will. He recognized, as we do, that there must be warmth as well as light for truth to be most effective. A sense of oughtness must be developed. As W. A. Squires says: "He dealt with life in its entirety, not merely with the thought process of his pupils. He nurtured the emotional life as well as the intellectual life of his disciples."[1] To this end he sought to arouse in-

---

[1] *The Pedagogy of Jesus in the Twilight of Today,* p. 137, George H. Doran Co., New York, 1927.

terest in topics as well as to convey information about
them. There were frequently on his lips the questions,
"What do you think?" (Matt. 18: 12) and "What do you
think of the Christ?" (Matt. 22: 42). As he thus induced
further meditation on a subject, interest was aroused
and conviction deepened. Also he appealed much to love,
the tender sentiment. A fine example is his effort to
deepen Peter's loyalty by raising thrice the question, "Do
you love me more than these?" (John 21: 15-17).

Likewise he appealed to fear and hate to deepen
conviction, including the fear of hell and hatred of sin.
Rewards and punishment were both emphasized. In discussing the judgment to come, he pictured some as cast
into outer darkness: "There men will weep and gnash
their teeth" (Matt. 25: 30).

In the light of such emphasis one cannot but feel that
the disciples went away from his teaching stirred to the
depths with a realization of the importance, as well as
the truthfulness, of the things he said. He developed
attitudes for or against matters presented. Here again
we will do well to follow his example, for if our teaching is to achieve results, pupils should go away from our
classes with a keen realization of the value of the thing
about which they have studied, and also a firm resolu-
tion to do something about it. Only this will give it the
purposeful emphasis so greatly needed in a time when
even sacred matters are taken lightly, if not even
laughed off with a joke. Teaching should strengthen
rather than weaken conviction. Youth must be fortified
within so as to be able to live good lives in an evil environment. When Rudyard Kipling's father took his son
on a boat trip and was informed that the boy had
climbed out over the water and would suffer certain death
if he let go, the old gentleman answered: "But that boy
will not let go." We should develop in our pupils conviction so strong that they will not let go.

III. CONVERT TO GOD [1]

The first major task of a teacher is to relate the pupil properly to God. It is the individual's initial religious act, and the most important one. Since learning is not thorough without response, so teaching about religion is not complete until one responds to God. One can never be rightly related to himself or to others until he is rightly related to God. It is the only basis for genuinely integrating or unifying life. Just as the magnetic needle quivers until it points to the north so the individual is unsettled until related to Christ. Josh Billings was right in saying, "We can never have an honest horse race until we have an honest human race." Righteousness will come only as people are converted to God. It is the basis of all moral progress.

All of life's activities must be directed from this center. It is life's greatest adjustment. "The soul of all culture is the culture of the soul." The Catholics are correct in saying that problems such as sex can be solved only in the light of the fear and love of God. Such is also true of temperance and world peace. So Christ said: "Seek first his kingdom and his righteousness, and all these things shall be yours as well" (Matt. 6: 33). He also said: "Unless you repent [change your mind] you will all likewise perish" (Luke 13: 3). And he told the cultured Nicodemus, "Unless one is born anew [from above], he cannot see the kingdom of God" (John 3: 3). So Christ sought first to get people converted to God, and until it is accomplished that is our greatest task as teachers.

This conversion experience is spoken of as a birth, a resurrection, an enlightment, a new heart, a change of

---

[1] For further discussion see Price, J. M., *Personal Factors in Character Building*, p. 121f, Baptist Sunday School Board, Nashville, 1934.

mind. It may vary in form as to temperament, age, culture and degree of sinfulness, but in all cases it involves the harmonious relating of the human to the divine personality. It may be a quiet experience or of the upheaval type; may come suddenly or gradually; may be dominantly intellectual, emotional, or volitional; and may be more of a getting away from sin, or more of a reaching out toward righteousness. In any case there is a committal to God and a crossing of the line into the Christian life.

Out of conversion come new motives, new interests, and new activities. "You shall love the Lord your God with all your heart, and with all your soul, with all your mind, and with all your strength" (Mark 12: 30). It is the experience that changes the world. "The converted Hottentot in Africa is nearer to the center of life than the most cultured pagan in America."

Governor Joseph W. Folk's mother was right when she said: "I was not a bit prouder of Joe the day he was inaugurated governor than I was the day he joined a Baptist church." Every Sunday school teacher should teach, pray, and work to the end that every pupil submit his life to God at the earliest possible moment. Each one, like the prodigal, should be led to say: "I will arise and go to my father" (Luke 15: 18).

IV. Relate to Others

Christian living involves the right relation to man as well as to God. In fact, both are wrapped up in the same experience. When Jesus was summarizing the first commandment, he added along with our relation to God, "You shall love your neighbor as yourself" (Mark 12: 31). When he stressed the doctrine of reward in eternity, he indicated that it was based on giving meat to the hungry, water to the thirsty, clothes to the naked, and showing kindness to the stranger, the sick, and the im-

prisoned (Matt. 25: 35-36). John went so far as to say:
"If any one says 'I love God', and hates his brother, he is
a liar" (1 John 4: 20).

That means that we are converted as social beings
rather than as independent selves. We are to be in harmony with man as well as with God. Henry C. King
once said: "Religion is knit up with all human relations
and tendencies and strivings, inextricably involved in
them all. And we shall look for its glory not in majestic
isolation, but rather in its ability to permeate and domi-
nate all life." Jesus sought to bring people into harmony
with one another as well as to convert them to God, and
he expects us to do likewise.

Several things were involved in this task of bringing
people into the right relations to one another. For one
thing Jesus emphasized the gospel of love, as the commandment previously mentioned indicates. He went so
far as to say: "You love one another; even as I have
loved you" (John 13: 34). He realized that genuine love
would break down all barriers. He cautioned against
hate, even saying: "Pray for those who persecute you"
(Matt. 5: 44). There could be no right relations where
hate reigned. In fact it is the starting point to murder.
One of his strongest emphases was on peacemaking.
"Blessed are the peacemakers, for they shall be called
the sons of God" (Matt. 5: 9). On sex purity he said:
"Every one who looks at a woman lustfully has already
committed adultery with her in his heart" (Matt.
5: 28).

His attitude and emphases would help to do away with
liquor, keep down race prejudice, settle problems between capital and labor, and eliminate war. If peaceful
relations ever come in these spheres, they will come not
through high-collared diplomats drinking intoxicating
toasts around a conference table, but as the Sunday
school and other teachers of the world build into growing

youth the right attitudes toward those of every clime, color, class, and creed.[1]

V. Meet Life Problems

In all of his teaching Jesus was not unmindful of the inner problems of his hearers, and was ever seeking to solve them and develop unified and happy disciples. "His teaching is essentially and wholly occasional . . . elicited by daily and hourly emergencies of contact and conversation and incident."[2] His was a life-centered rather than a material-centered emphasis. Apart from the Teaching on the Mount, most of his recorded sayings were directed toward helping persons meet specific issues they confronted. He did not even use such general terms as religious, spiritual, ethical, and conscientious, but rather stressed particular virtues. In fact it is likely that as he set forth the beatitudes there were those before him wrestling with the problems of pride, impurity, sorrow, and the like.

Just as the old Latin teacher said that he did not teach Latin but boys, so the Master did not teach truth but persons, and the Scriptures and other materials were merely means to this end. Even the verse of Scripture which stresses inspiration says that it is not an end in itself, but rather the Scriptures are "profitable for teaching . . . that the man of God may be complete, equipped for every good work" (2 Tim. 3: 16-17). "His aim was always fixed upon the life, rather than upon the intellect."[3]

This emphasis is seen throughout his ministry. He quoted from twenty of the thirty-nine Old Testament

---

[1] For more extended discussion, see Price, J. M., *Vital Problems in Christian Living,* Ch. 8, Baptist Sunday School Board, Nashville, 1942.

[2] Curtis, W. A., *Jesus Christ the Teacher,* p. 75, Oxford University Press, 1943.

[3] Hitchcock, A. W., *The Psychology of Jesus,* p. 168, The Pilgrim Press, Boston, 1907.

books in his teaching and every time in relation to a
problem or situation causing his disciples difficulty.
When he dealt with the woman at the well, he probed
her life to reveal her need. As he confronted Nicodemus,
he put his finger on the weak spot in his formal Phari-
saical life and taught him a lesson on the necessity and
nature of regeneration. When the rich young ruler came
asking what to do to inherit eternal life, he questioned
until he discerned that his possessions were his main
problem, and then told him what to do about them.

Probably the outstanding instance is the request of the
man who wanted him to make his brother divide the inheritance, which was made right in the midst of his discourse of God's providential care. It was entirely out of
harmony with the occasion and the natural thing would
have been to ignore or rebuke him and go on with his
message. But the Master Teacher did neither. Perceiv-
ing the man's covetous heart he turned aside from his
discourse and gave him a lesson on life that has blessed
the world. As he pictured the prosperous farmer building
bigger barns and enjoying lavish means, the man was
forced to see his own covetous attitude (Luke 12: 13-21).

If there is any one emphasis that is needed above all
others in our Sunday school teaching today, it is that we
should not teach lessons but people. "Purposeful teaching
for purposeful living" should be every teacher's motto.
The teacher of adults who refused to allow a pupil to
ask a question because the time was short and "we
must cover the lesson," missed the main point in teaching. If necessary we should even turn aside from the
lesson to meet the need of a class. Many preachers do
that in their sermons. George W. Truett said once that
he preached an entire sermon for the benefit of one man
in the vast audience. But in doing so he likely met the
needs of many, just as Jesus helped humanity throughout the ages in turning from his formal message to meet

the needs of one covetous man. If we learn nothing else from this entire study on Jesus as a teacher, let us never forget that he taught to meet life needs.

VI. Grow Mature Character

Jesus' aims did not stop with securing a formal response to his teachings or even with meeting specific problems. He sought to go further and develop in his followers those graces which would enable them to overcome their weaknesses and vices and grow into strong, integrated Christian characters. Charles F. Kent puts his aims thus, "To save men from yielding to the temptations which come thick and fast to every man and woman; to help them to overcome the passions which swept over them; to save the haughty tax-collector from his greed; the woman of the streets from those influences that had laid an almost irresistible hold on her." [1] He sought to develop such positive virtues as honesty, humility, purity, unselfishness, kindness, and sacrifice which make for nobility of character, steadfastness in conduct, and joy in living. His ideal for his disciples was a life as nearly free from sin as was humanly possible.

Many instances bear out these statements. He denounced heartily the Pharisees who made an outward show of religion but inwardly were hypocrites. One of the most vivid word pictures he ever drew was of the boastful Pharisee bragging publicly in loud-sounding tones about his goodness, while the downcast publican asked God to be merciful to him a sinner. He discounted formal praying, fasting, and giving, and stressed the importance of proper attitudes of heart instead. He urged his followers to go further than the legal regulations of the law and the prophets, and to consider motives and purposes.

---

[1] *Great Teachers of Judaism and Christianity,* p. 116, Eaton and Mains, New York, 1911.

Anger as well as murder is blamable, and the lustful look as well as adultery itself is sinful. His disciples were to be as honest without an oath as with one, rise above vengeance even to turning the other cheek, and love their enemies as their friends. He indicated that Christian growth is like the plant, "first the blade, then the ear, then the full grain in the ear" (Mark 4: 28). He urged Peter to feed the lambs, the little sheep, and the sheep (John 21: 15-17). He recognized that, "Heaven is not reached by a single bound, but we build the ladder by which we rise from the lowly earth to the vaulted skies, and we mount to its summit round by round."

In order that their experience might be genuine, thorough, and permanent, the Master urged his hearers to count the cost carefully before following, to be sure that their love for him surpassed their affection for any earthly kin or object, to renounce all they had, and to take up their cross daily and follow him. He was more concerned about quality than quantity, about weighing people than counting them, about permanent results than temporary ones.

And if we are to follow his example, we must realize that it is more important to secure a genuine than an immediate response, that our work has barely begun when a pupil is converted, and that our task is to develop him "to mature manhood, to the measure of the stature of the fullness of Christ" (Eph. 4: 13). W. E. Hatcher well said: "It is at least as important to save what we have as to save the lost." And J. B. Gambrell stated: "Baptists have evangelized and they have baptized, but they have not taught, and out of that have come most of their troubles."

VII. TRAIN FOR SERVICE

The final task of the master Teacher was to train his disciples to carry his teachings around the world. Much of the latter part of his ministry was given to this task. They were so well prepared that they and their successors have won the largest number of followers of any group of religious teachers on earth. They were effective though they did not belong to the professional teaching group of scribes and rabbis. Nor did they have professional training, but after a brief period of preparation under Jesus they became the world's most significant teachers. The eleven, the seventy, and others started the message on its worldwide march, and it has not stopped to this day. Their teaching has girdled the globe, and changed the course of history.

Several elements entered into this training. He said to his disciples, "Follow me, and I will make you fishers of men" (Matt. 4: 19). Also, "He appointed twelve, to be with him, and to be sent out to preach" (Mark 3: 14). The first and probably the greatest aspect of their training was personal association with him and learning through example and imitation. They saw him as he sympathized, comforted, fed, and healed, and they caught his spirit. The second phase was through listening to his matchless teaching under varied circumstances and a wide range of subjects. They learned through "the hearing of the ear." And finally, he gave them practice work by having them do the baptizing. Also he sent out the twelve on a teaching tour, then the seventy on a similar mission. And when they returned, he called them together for a report on their work, thus giving guidance and supervision.

So they learned by example, precept, and practice. No group of teachers ever had better training. When they were finally ready, he sent them forth saying, "Make disciples of all nations, baptizing them in the name of the Father and of the Son and of the Holy Spirit, teaching them to observe all that I have commanded you" (Matt. 28: 19-20). Never did so much depend upon so few, or that few give such a fine account of their stewardship.

As teachers we should recognize that the training of others constitutes one of our tasks. Out of our classes today must come the Sunday school, Training Union, W.M.U., and other volunteer leaders for our churches tomorrow. Likewise from these classes must come the future pastors, educational directors, student workers, foreign missionaries, and other religious leaders. While it does not express all of the truth to say that we are saved to serve, yet undoubtedly that is a part of everyone's responsibility. Each worker, therefore, should be trained and the Sunday school teacher is responsible for a part of the task.

In the light of all the facts it is marvelous how broad and far-reaching were the aims of Jesus. They comprehended every phase of human nature—thought, feeling, and will. They included all of one's relationships—to his body, to others, and to God. They covered every phase of his activity—personal, domestic, ecclesiastical, and professional. In short he sought "a perfect man in a perfect society." And the realization of these aims would mean the bringing in of the kingdom of God on the earth.

TEACHING AIDS

BLACKBOARD OUTLINE

    I. Form right ideals
   II. Fix strong convictions
  III. Convert to God
  IV. Relate to others
    V. Meet life problems
  VI. Grow mature character
 VII. Train for service

TOPICS FOR DISCUSSION

1. Show the significance of ideals.
2. What does conviction add to truth?
3. Why is response necessary to learning?
4. How can we insure world peace?
5. State some life problems of the class you teach.
6. What was wrong with the religion of the Pharisees?
7. Which of Jesus' methods of training was most effective? Why?

CHAPTER IV

Principles Underlying His Work

AT FIRST GLANCE it may not appear that the teaching ministry of Jesus was rooted in any particular principle. Rather it may seem to be a sort of spontaneous activity without any definite underlying philosophy. However, such is not the case. It was far from being a haphazard process. The more one studies his work the more it is evident that it was grounded in substantial principles. To be sure they are not stated in so many words. But they are there nevertheless, and stand out as one examines his work. We shall notice some of them.

I. TOOK THE LONG LOOK

It is evident that Jesus took the long look in selecting his helpers. Seeing from the altitude of God he could discern in them what neither they nor their associates could. He looked at their future possibilities and not merely their present qualifications. For example he saw in the impulsive, radical, vacillating Simon a strong, courageous, stalwart character and gave him the name of Peter (stone). Likewise he perceived in the youthful, uncharitable John ("son of thunder") a much more considerate and lovable character, even the "beloved disciple." He could see in a proud Pharisee or an outcast woman possibilities that others did not discern. Says Bruce Barton: "The people saw in Zaccheus merely a dishonest little Jew; he saw in him a man of unusual generosity. . . . So with Matthew—the crowd saw only a despised tax collector, Jesus saw the potential writer of a book which will live forever." [1]

As the artist sees the prospective picture on the canvas and the sculptor the future statue in the uncarved stone, so the Master saw in each pupil the personality that was to be and worked optimistically and patiently to bring this image to realization. "He never seems to have despaired of any man. There was always hope for the worst and the weakest of them." [2]

Jesus also took the long look at the task of developing character, knowing that it requires time to shape ideals, form attitudes, and develop habits. As Maltbie D. Babcock has said: "Good habits are not made on birthdays, nor Christian character at the New Year. The vision may dawn, the dream may waken, the heart leap with new inspiration on some mountaintop, but the test, the triumph, is at the foot of the mountain on the level plain." A mushroom grows up overnight but it requires a decade to develop an oak. This viewpoint is seen in the parable of the seed sown on the earth which springs up and develops from the blade to the full grain in the ear (Mark 4: 28). Also in the admonition to Peter to feed his lambs and grow them into sheep (John 21: 15-17).

Jesus knew that the kingdom of God would come not by whirlwind campaigns and highly wrought occasions, but by the steady process of teaching and training, "precept upon precept—line upon line." Only thus will the immature Christian attain the fulness of stature of Christian manhood. This long look gave him steadfastness. "When he was blocked in one direction, he patiently and serenely turned in another. When he was blocked in all directions and nothing was left to him but to die, he did

---

[1] *The Man Nobody Knows,* p. 25, The Bobbs-Merrill Co., Indianapolis, 1928.
[2] Hitchcock, A. W., *The Psychology of Jesus,* p. 173, The Pilgrim Press, Boston, 1907.

it as sweetly and confidently as he fed the multitudes by the sea." [1] He was sure of the results.

Taking the long look as to our pupils' possibilities and the task involved in character building will likewise help to keep us from being pessimistic. We will not be as Woodrow Wilson's father, who said: "I am afraid my son Woodrow will not amount to much." Nor as the evangelist who, at the close of the revival in which George Truett and others were converted, felt that the meeting had largely failed since few adults were won. Nor the church leaders who hesitated to recommend D. L. Moody for church membership.

Rather we will regard each pupil as having unlimited possibilities. Likewise we will look upon our teaching not as a burdensome task but as a glorious opportunity—the most effective human means of developing character. We will see with Von Humboldt that what we are to have in our civilization tomorrow we must put into our schools today, and with Robert Wells Veach that social progress is a battle between schoolmasters. We will realize that "the teacher is indeed the keeper of the gates of tomorrow."

II. STRESSED THE PERSONAL TOUCH

The tendency today is to seek to accomplish results through mass meeting activities. We are obsessed with numbers. The success of an evangelist, a pastor, or a minister of education is measured by the number of converts, membership of the church, or size of the school. Drives of one kind or another are the order of the day. Like Gregory the Illuminator, Xavier, and other ambitious missionaries we want to win people in droves. So the emphasis is more on the crowd than on the individual.

---

[1] Marquis, John A., *Learning to Teach from the Master Teacher,* p. 59, The Westminster Press, Philadelphia, 1913.

This does not coincide with the best educational procedure, and is likely to bring superficial and temporary results. Through the years it has been the cause of a great deal of spurious experience and falling away. A larger per cent of converts who are won in regular services hold out than of those won in revivals. This emphasis accounts in part for the difference between the number of members on church rolls and the number who are dependable. It contributes also to doubt and defections from the faith. J. R. Graves once said that every prominent atheist he had known had at some time made a profession of faith.

Jesus' emphasis was different. He stressed the personal touch. "For the most part His time was spent with individuals or the group designated as disciples or pupils."[1] To be sure he did deal with crowds. People followed him from Capernaum, Jerusalem, Decapolis, and other places. Sometimes they numbered four or five thousand. He sympathized with them, spoke to them, fed them, and healed them. At times his activity took on much of the appearance of a great popular movement, especially after certain acts of healing and during his triumphal entry.

But he did not encourage mass following. In fact he was rather disturbed by it, sought to slip away from the throngs, and restrained group response. When great multitudes followed him, he told them they must love him more than their loved ones in order to be true followers (Luke 14: 25-27). He knew the fickleness of crowds and the superficiality of group response, realizing full well that "those who bless you today may curse you tomorrow." So his main service was not rendered in mass meeting activities. "The Master was evidently more concerned that a few people should thoroughly

---

[1] Benson, C. H., *History of Christian Education*, p. 30, The Moody Press, Chicago, 1943.

understand him and be filled with his spirit than that
great multitudes should follow him in a superficial
manner." [1]

With only a little more than three years in which to
do his work he spent much of his time in dealing with
individuals. The most striking instances of his ministry
took place in such activities. "The method of Jesus for
redeeming this world was not to wait for great occasions
or for some dramatic moment. Rather it was to utilize
any opportunity that came to him, in the most ordinary,
commonplace, and out-of-the-way events of everyday
life, and then give all that was most precious to the one
soul that needed it." [2]

Among persons dealt with were Nicodemus, Zaccheus,
the woman of Samaria, the woman taken in adultery,
the man with an inheritance, the rich young ruler, the
critical lawyer, and the nobleman of Capernaum. Horne
lists a total of about sixty. As he confronted these he
had better opportunity for understanding their needs and
counseling them. The mass leader has been compared
by Dean Inge to a man dashing a bucket of water at a
group of narrow-necked vessels hoping some will go in.
The personal counselor deals with specific cases. Jesus
realized the superiority of the latter. As H. H. Horne
says: "He worked by preference and most successfully
with individuals because of the very nature of crowds.
He did not trust crowds nor himself to them as he trusted
individuals." [3]

The teacher today should be a personal counselor,
guiding people in the solution of their problems. In his
teaching he should have a class of such size as to know
the needs of individual members and teach accord-

---

[1] McCoy, Charles F., *The Art of Jesus as a Teacher*, p. 146. The
Judson Press, Philadelphia, 1930.
[2] Calkins, Raymond, *How Jesus Dealt with Men*, p. 58, Abingdon-
Cokesbury Press, New York, 1942.
[3] *Jesus the Master Teacher*, pp. 142, 143, Association Press, New
York, 1925.

ingly. One teacher kept a class record with detailed information from parents, associates, and public school teachers, and prepared and presented each lesson in the light of these facts. Said a prominent preacher: "George Truett was great when he preached from his pulpit, greater when he spoke to the Southern Baptist Convention from the Capitol steps in Washington, greater still when he addressed the Baptist World Alliance in Atlanta, but greatest of all when he stood in a country cemetery and comforted a little girl who had lost her mother."

III. BEGAN WHERE PEOPLE WERE

Jesus did not give prepared addresses on formal occasions. Whether in the home, the synagogue, the mountain or by the sea he taught naturally and informally, starting with the pupil's interest and needs. "He began not with formulated beliefs, subject matter, tradition or even the Bible, but with living persons where they were in their experience of life." [1] "He did not take a passage from the law or the prophets, unravel its general principles, and then look about to discover if there were some place where those principles might be having an immediate application. Rather did he address himself to the human situation before him." [2] He took persons as they were and sought to lead them where he wanted them to go. This is in line with Thorndike's "Law of Readiness" which states that when a person is ready to act in a certain way to do so is satisfying and to be prevented is annoying.

When a lawyer asked what to do to inherit eternal life, Jesus referred him to his law (Luke 10: 25-26). In his conversation with the wicked woman at Jacob's well he

---

[1] Bower, W. C., *Christ and Christian Education*, p. 20, Abingdon-Cokesbury Press, Nashville, 1943.
[2] Day, George, E., *Christ and Human Personality*, p. 249, The Abingdon Press, New York, 1934.

began with "water," the thing in which she was interested, and led on to "living water" (John 4: 10). As he stood up in the synagogue to read and announce his ministry, he started with the familiar passage in Isaiah capitalizing on the expectation of the Messiah (Luke 4: 16-30). By these means he had the attention and interest. "No formal program or prescribed curriculum got in the way of his helping his disciples to learn." [1]

Beginning where the pupil is means not only starting with his interests and needs, but also using language familiar to him. It is based on the old law of "apperception" which once had considerable emphasis and needs it still. Literally it means ad-perception, or adding to one's perceptions. The idea is that the pupil learns new truths through old ones, or goes from the known to the unknown. "The truth to be taught must be learned through truth already known." This is the customary approach in learning.

A little boy having seen the picture of an alligator, called the first lizard he saw by that name. A colored laundress watching a Red Cross nurses' parade remarked that she never saw so much "white wash." A Southern child seeing his first snow falling, called the snowflakes feathers. Since we learn new truths through old it is important to select language and imagery familiar to the pupil. Otherwise the idea does not carry over. Jesus used words that were common such as "light," "salt," "bread," and "meat," and referred to things that were familiar such as "soils," "vineyards," "sheep," and "leaven."

It might be noticed in passing that the times when he was most misunderstood were when he used terminology that had another meaning to his hearers than the one intended. When he used the term "new birth," Nicodemus, cultured though he was, immediately thought of a

[1] Richardson, N. E., *The Christ of the Classroom*, p. 26, The Macmillan Co., New York, 1931.

physical birth. When he spoke of his "kingdom," his hearers pictured an earthly throne like David's and control by force, rather than a spiritual rule in human hearts. When he said that if his "temple" were destroyed, in three days he would raise it up, it seems not to have occurred to his disciples that he meant his body. So it is not only very important to start with experiences and problems familiar to pupils, but to see to it that they understand clearly the language and the illustrations used. Dr. Gambrell once told of a preacher who spent three minutes giving an illustration and eighteen explaining what he meant by it.

IV. STAYED WITH VITAL MATTERS

In all of Jesus' teaching there is no indication that he dealt with secondary or incidental matters to any appreciable extent. He did not teach the rudiments of learning nor the history, geography, or customs of Palestine. He did not give much emphasis to organization, equipment, or materials. Neither did he set forth elaborate systems of doctrine to be drilled into future generations. The nearest approach to that is the Teaching on the Mount which can be read in half an hour. He did not even stress memorization of Scripture, comments on Scripture, or matters of theological discussion as did the scribes in their teaching in the synagogues. Instead of these things the Teacher dealt with vital problems— matters that pertained definitely to moral and religious living.

The Master well knew that the issues of life grow out of the fundamental instincts such as the preservative, reproductive, projective, and social. He himself had been tempted at most of these points, and realized that the perversion of these drives brings on the sins of society. The matter of human nature is the chief problem we face. So he sought to regulate life problems at their

source. Consequently he warned his followers against
the covetous spirit which is the outgrowth and perversion
of the urge for self preservation. He counseled against
the lustful look, growing out of the reproductive instinct,
and urged his disciples to be pure in heart. He discouraged that outgrowth of the projective drive which
seeks to have the prominent place and lord it over others.
And he strongly denounced pride and vain display which
are perversions of the social instinct. In thus staying
with vital issues he gave a gentle rebuke to Sunday school
teachers who spend their time on incidental matters.

In discussing vital issues Jesus did not spend his time
merely in denouncing the issues of the day as people
sometimes do. His was by no means a negative approach
or merely a gospel of "quit your meanness." This sort
of thing does not last, as he showed very definitely in
the story of the expelled evil spirit returning to the
empty house and taking possession again (Matt. 12: 43-
45). Rather he recognized the necessity of a positive
approach. In other words there must be a new dynamic,
"the expulsive power of a new affection." Consequently
he sought to show the covetous inheritor that life is more
than possessions, and the sordid Samaritan woman that
there were higher satisfactions than the physical. He
made religion a vital and dynamic thing. "With Jesus
life was something more than the adjustment of an or-
ganism to its immediate environment. He had in mind
a strong and unified personality that would meet any
test."[1] "Jesus thought of religion as a quality of life,
diffused throughout the person's interests and activities
. . . never a specialized interest apart from the rest of
life. He spoke only in terms of divine-human relationships."[2]

[1] Squires, W. A., *The Pedagogy of Jesus in the Twilight of Today*,
p. 243, Geo. H. Doran Co., New York, 1927.
[2] Bower, W. C., *Christ and Christian Education*, pp. 22-23, The
Abingdon-Cokesbury Press, Nashville, 1943.

V. WORKED ON THE CONSCIENCE

The scribes and Pharisees, who were the professional religious teachers of the day, sought to develop character largely through minute regulations. "Christ came to a people for whom religion involved the acceptance of an elaborate code of rules, and fixed times and modes of worship."[1] These rules covered minutely almost every phase of life and burdened the people down. There were forty-two on the one insignificant matter of what kind of knot it was allowable to tie on the sabbath. Moral and religious living was almost intolerable under such a system. Jesus knew the futility of such external procedures and sought to free the people from a virtual slavery to them. Consequently he cried out against them saying: "You load men with burdens hard to bear" (Luke 11: 46). A positive, dynamic emphasis was needed if people were to be motivated sufficiently to meet the issues of life. This he sought to give to his disciples.

Also as previously indicated the Master recognized the inadequacy of responses that were dominantly emotional and without sufficient convictions to back them up. He knew full well that pathetic stories and appeals to pride are not adequate motives. So he did not resort to them. Never once did he ask a person to raise the hand, sign a pledge, or stand up as an evidence of acceptance. Neither did he ask them to clasp his hand, though he did urge them to follow him. "He never compels or dictates, never forces assent, never imposes his teaching dogmatically."[2] Life decisions are too serious to be made lightly. He wanted responses that would be permanent, decisions that were adequately motivated.

[1] Raven, Charles E., *Christ and Modern Education,* p. 107, Henry Holt and Co., New York, 1928.
[2] Raven, Charles E., *Christ and Modern Education,* pp. 104-5, Henry Holt and Co., New York, 1928.

For him there must be no short-cut methods. Better no
response at all than one that is spurious.

So Jesus made his appeal to the conscience which is
one's sense of moral obligation or sensitivity to right and
wrong. "These you ought to have done," said he to the
hypocritical scribes and Pharisees (Matt. 23: 23), and in
reprimanding the man who hid his talent he said: "You
ought" (Matt. 25: 27). He worked on the conscience
more than the intellect. He not only risked his cause on
a teaching procedure but also rested his case with an
enlightened conscience. And results have justified the
principle. He made truth both clear and compelling.
People went away from his teaching feeling that something should be done about it. Horne says: "Jesus without a social system has been more influential in
reshaping society than those with a social system because
he gives a social conscience which transforms society." [1]
And Hinsdale adds: "The calm confidence with which he
rests on moral means is the grandest tribute that has
ever been paid to human nature." [2] It is likewise about
the grandest tribute to his teaching.

Here is a principle that we need to stress more and
more if we are to make our teaching effective and permanent. This is true whether we are seeking conversions,
financial pledges, or volunteers for religious work. It
preserves freedom and prevents superficiality. It is definitely better than minute regulations. Dr. Gambrell
once said to his younger colleagues in a faculty meeting:
"After a while you will learn that you cannot do everything by rules and regulations." He was right. Neither
can we by an emotional appeal only. Widespread back-
sliding and falling down on pledges bear witness to that
fact. Conscience must be enlightened and aroused. We

---

[1] *The Philosophy of Christian Education*, p. 98, Fleming H. Revell
Co., New York, 1937.
[2] *Jesus as a Teacher*, p. 233, The Christian Publishing Co., St.
Louis, 1895.

must not pressure people into doing what they do not want to do, but rather work on their "wanters." Responses must come from a sense of moral obligation.

VI. DREW OUT THE BEST

Some people have a way of drawing out the worst that is in the other person. The attitude they take and the approach they make seem somehow to elicit an unfavorable response. They cause the one with whom they deal to build up a barrier and a resistance. Frequently even an antagonistic spirit is developed. And this may be done by well-meaning persons who are seeking to do the right thing, but lack discernment and judgment. A college schoolmate whom the writer led to Christ said after his conversion, "I would have done this long before had not certain ones come to me." This drawing out of the worst may happen in enlisting pupils for a class, in instructing them in class, and in trying to lead them into service as well as in winning them to Christ. It may come about because of a failure to understand the pupil, a distant and unsympathetic attitude, lack of judgment and tact, or as a result of a critical and caustic spirit. In any case it drives a pupil further away and does more harm than good.

With Jesus it was different. Somehow he was able to draw out the best that was in people. Whether it was a self-righteous Pharisee, an unscrupulous tax collector, or a fallen woman, he appealed to the finer nature and elicited the good. Not only was this true of those who had gone far into sin, but also of those merely immature. He seems almost to have specialized in taking unlikely persons and making them into splendid characters, as he did with the eleven.

He did it by stressing their future possibilities, showing an interest in them, and inspiring them to achieve the good. "He believed that the way to get faith out of men is to show that you have faith in them, and from that great principle of executive management he never ceased." [1] When he showed what faith the size of a mustard seed could accomplish, when he told the adulterous woman that he did not condemn her and to sin no more, and when he said to his disciples that they were the salt of the earth, he was implanting hope and confidence that would draw out every ounce of effort to meet his expectation.

One of the most important things we can do as Sunday school teachers is to seek to draw out the best in our pupils. There is no one so seemingly hopeless but that there are possibilities in him. And there is no one so mean but that has something in him to which an appeal can be made. When someone asked a woman suffrage speaker on Boston Common who would protect her from a threatening mob she pointed to the ring leader and said: "This gentleman will protect me, and see that I have a chance to be heard." And the so-called "gentleman" did that very thing.

When the superintendent of the Rhode Island Reform School learned that a boy was planning to run away and go home, he furnished him car fare for a week-end trip home, and trusted him to return even when both the boy and his mother declared he would not. He returned. Mrs. Jessie Burral Eubank built a class of 1,600 nonresident girls in Washington in wartime largely by inspiring them to their best with the motto, "We specialize on the wholly impossible." We must put our confidence, our optimism, and our inspiration against the doubt, the discouragement, and the defeat of our pupils and draw out the best in their lives. We cannot do this unless we can see something of the latent possibilities within them.

---

[1] Barton, Bruce, *The Man Nobody Knows,* p. 28, The Bobbs-Merrill Co., Indianapolis, 1925.

VII. SECURED PUPIL'S SELF-ACTIVITY

One of the famous "Seven Laws of Teaching" by John M. Gregory is, "Excite and direct the self-activities of the learner, and tell him nothing he can learn for himself."[1] It is based on the fact that learning does not take place without mental activity. "Saints are not made during sleep," said Thomas Carlyle. Neither is a scholar. L. A. Weigle says: "Not what you tell a pupil, but what he thinks as a result of your words; not what you do for him, but what he does for himself; not the impression, but the reaction upon it—determines his development. You cannot put ideas into the pupil's head; your words are but symbols of the ideas that are in your own. He must interpret the symbols and from them construct his own ideas. Teaching succeeds only insofar as it enlists the activity of the pupil."[2]

The learner should not merely sit still while the teacher instills. His mind must be active. A three-cycle movement is necessary—intellectual knowledge, emotional stirring, and volitional response. The pupil learns self-denial only by practicing it, and the joy of giving by trying it. So storytelling, lecturing, and visual aids are not enough. Discussion, dramatization, and service projects must be engaged in. We learn to do by doing.

This principle the Master thoroughly recognized and acted upon. "Rather than give ready-made solutions Jesus threw people back on their own resources."[3] He was stressing this principle when he said: "If any man's will is to do his will, he shall know" (John 7: 17). He stressed it further when he likened hearing only to build-

---

[1] *The Seven Laws of Teaching,* p. 82, The Pilgrim Press, Boston, 1886.
[2] *The Teacher,* p. 87, American Baptist Publication Society, Philadelphia, 1917.
[3] Bower, W. C., *Christ and Christian Education,* p. 24, Abingdon-Cokesbury Press, Nashville, 1943.

ing a house on the sand, and hearing and responding to building on a rock. The main point in the parable of the talents is that the one who uses his powers develops them, and the one who does not, loses them. In the parable of the soils he teaches that it is the response to the seed that counts.

He had the disciples do the baptizing for him, and sent them and others out on missions of teaching and healing. The disciples were asked to distribute the food in feeding the five thousand, and to roll away the stone at the raising of Lazarus. The blind man must wash his eyes in the pool of Siloam before receiving sight, and the rich ruler sell all and give to the poor in order to have eternal life. Among activities mentioned are "arise," "come," "follow," "go," "wash," "do," "watch," "offer," "preach," "teach," "disciple," "feed." His was a gospel of thought and action as well as of hearing and feeling.

TEACHING AIDS

BLACKBOARD OUTLINE

I. Took the long look
II. Stressed the personal touch
III. Began where people were
IV. Stayed with vital matters
V. Worked on the conscience
VI. Drew out the best
VII. Secured pupil's self-activity

TOPICS FOR DISCUSSION

1. Show the value of discovering pupils' possibilities.
2. Why did Jesus prefer individuals rather than crowds?
3. Discuss the principle of apperception.
4. What are the most vital things to stress?
5. Give your definition of conscience.
6. How secure a student's self-activity?

CHAPTER V

His Use of Materials

JESUS' use of materials in teaching is one of the very interesting and revealing phases of our study. And it may prove to be a very suggestive and helpful one if we can see in the materials he used suggestions as to those that we may utilize in our own work. They vary as to sources, kinds, and uses. In no sense was he a slave to them or dependent on them. Rather as they passed through the crucible of his own mind, he put his creative thinking into them and made them over.

I. SOURCES

There are several general sources from which the Master drew in his teaching. These might be broken down into further subdivisions. They grew out of his training and experience, and were drawn upon as needed. Only brief, general references can be made to them in the space allotted. It would take an entire book for thorough treatment.

1. *The Scriptures*

It is very evident that Jesus used the Old Testament Scriptures freely. D. R. Piper says that he gave thirty-eight direct quotations, four allusions to some Scripture event, and fifty times used language paralleling words of the Old Testament. He referred to twenty-one of the Old Testament books.[1] The Psalms and Deuteronomy seem

[1] *How Would Jesus Teach?* p. 49, David C. Cook Publishing Co., Elgin, 1931.

to have been used most. His thought is thoroughly permeated by Old Testament ideas and cast in Old Testament language.

Sometimes he gave direct quotations such as, "Man shall not live by bread alone, but by every word that proceeds from the mouth of God" (Matt. 4: 4; Deut. 8: 9). There are many such passages. Without attempting to be complete, Horne lists thirty-three direct quotations.[1] Many of them refer definitely to Jesus and to his activities and therefore are doubly effective. They carried both the weight of the Master and that of the Old Testament.

In some instances he made statements that were practically identical with Old Testament Scriptures without indicating that they were quotations. In Matthew 5: 5 we find the statement, "Blessed are the meek, for they shall inherit the earth," and in Psalm 37: 11, we read, "The meek shall inherit the earth." There are around forty of these parallel passages in the Old and New Testaments. Evidently he had assimilated them so as to give them in substance.

In other cases he alluded to the Scriptures without definitely quoting from them. There are a number of these, such as his statement regarding it being more tolerable for Sodom and Gomorrah in the judgment than for those of his day (Matt. 10: 15). Another was the very brief mention of the instance of Lot's wife looking back (Luke 17: 32), and an implied caution that his followers should not do the same. Such references were about as effective as definite quotations.

He made some references that are difficult to locate such as, "These are days of vengeance, to fulfill all that is written" (Luke 21: 22). Apparently he saw in the Scriptures some things which we do not. Also, he seems

[1] *Jesus the Master Teacher*, pp. 93ff, Association Press, New York, 1920.

to have been familiar with extrabiblical Jewish writings for we find statements similar to this: "Forgive thy neighbour the hurt that he hath done unto thee, so shall thy sins also be forgiven when thou prayest" (Ecclesiasticus 28: 2. Apocrypha). (Cf. Matt. 6: 12, 14).

Teachers today will do well to profit by the example of Jesus, and familiarize themselves with the history, teaching, and even words of the Bible, and use the material constantly. The Bible is God's word, and people believe it, like to hear it, and no other material can be used with such weight. This necessitates a thorough study and mastery of the entire Bible as well as the particular portions used in the Sunday school lessons. One of our greatest weaknesses has been piece-meal study and teaching of the Word of God.

2. *Natural World*

It is evident from his teaching that Jesus was a close observer of the forces of nature and made considerable use of them in his work. "We see the blossoming vineyards; the valley gay with roses and lilies, the orchards of pomegranates; the flocks feeding in the pastures, the doves nesting in the clefts of the rocks, the foxes making havoc of the vineyards. . . . We smell the perfume of spikenard, frankincense, and cedars of Lebanon. We hear the hum of bees, the bleating of sheep and goats, the cooing of the wood-pigeon." [1] He seems to have been familiar with every phase of nature. This knowledge of nature came in handy in his teaching. As Wilson says: "His habitual speech was colored, dyed, steeped in the beauty of the earth about Him and of the sky above Him." He lived close to nature and absorbed much from it which he called forth in his teaching in later years.

In the heavens above he observed the wind blowing

---

[1] Quoted by Wilson, Harold, *Jesus at School*, p. 18, The National Sunday School Union, London.

where it would, the sun shining on the evil and the good, the rain falling on the just and the unjust, the storm beating on the house. In the vegetable realm he discerned the vital relation of the vine and the branches, the horror of the barren fig tree, the growth of corn from blade to ear, the presence of tares among the wheat. In bird life he saw the harmless dove, the raven seeking food, the sparrow falling to the ground, the eagle circling over its prey. In animal life he noted the deadly viper, the ox in the ditch, the fox stalking its prey, the dog licking sores. All of these made their impression on him, became a part of him, and were available for use in teaching.

These things entered into his parables particularly. There are four dealing with animals—sheep, goats, dogs, and eagles; seven dealing with plants, including leaven, tares, fig tree, and mustard seed; and sixteen dealing with things, such as light, soil, dragnet, and hidden treasure. Many other references and illustrations came from these sources and greatly enlivened his instruction. Any teaching will be more effective with illustrations drawn from nature, particularly if they are familiar to the hearers and are wisely chosen. It is difficult to think what Jesus would have done without such material, or how we can do without it, especially with children and others living close to nature. One reason J. B. Gambrell is remembered so well is that he drew many of his illustrations from the realm of nature and everyday life. They caught the attention of the masses, were readily remembered by them, and have influenced their thinking ever since.

3. *Current Affairs*

The Master Teacher was likewise alert to the situations arising in the lives of those around him. He was familiar with the bushel measure, the water pot, the skin of wine; lighting a lamp, patching clothes, grinding at a mill; the widow's mite, brothers' quarrels, children at play. While he did not draw from secular history, philosophy, or poetry he did make considerable use of current events. In other words he never missed an opportunity to seize on every occasion as it arose to impart his precepts. "He found in the common events of everyday life the inspiration for the most profound and inspiring themes that have ever filled the human heart." [1]

He drew lessons from the hen protecting her brood, a woman kneading dough, the farmer sowing seed, the vineyard keeper pruning vines, the fisherman catching fish, the builder constructing a house, the tailor sewing a patch on an old garment, the king making preparation to go to war. Apparently nothing escaped his watchful eye. And he turned these experiences to good account in his teaching. "He spoke with authority—the authority of actual experience—and not as the scribes, who depended on the libraries." [2]

Many other instances could be given of this use of occasions. When he went into the Temple and found it polluted by the traders, he not only taught a lesson by driving them out, but he used the incident to stress the sacredness of God's house. When the Pharisees complained that his disciples were violating the sabbath by plucking grain to eat as they went through the fields, he took the opportunity to give a much needed emphasis on the purpose of the sabbath. When the scribes and Pharisees criticized him for eating with publicans and sinners, he told the stories of the anxious search for the lost coin, sheep, and boy to help them see the proper attitude toward the needy.

He even went outside his own circle in the use of current happenings showing familiarity with world affairs

---

[1] McCoy, C. F., *The Art of Jesus as a Teacher,* p. 56, The Judson Press, Philadelphia, 1930.
[2] Wilson, P. W., *The Christ We Forget,* p. 71, Fleming H. Revell Co., New York, 1917.

around him. While stressing the necessity of repentance
he told of the Galileans whose blood Pilate had mingled
with their sacrifices, and of the falling of the tower of
Siloam killing eighteen people. In each instance he added
that these people were not worse sinners than Jerusalem's
citizens, and that unless they changed their minds they
likewise would perish (Luke 13: 1-5). Evidently he observed Herod's doings rather closely for he referred to
him as "that fox." This use of current experiences had
much to do in making his teaching life-centered, interesting, and effective.

All of this shows that a curriculum does not consist
solely of textbooks or special assignments, but of other
materials as well. The inventive teacher will draw from
many sources and thus greatly enrich his teaching. The
more he knows about current affairs the better it will be.
Especially valuable also are books containing brief bi-
ographies, good fiction, and history. If one can draw
illustrations from these sources he will be able to make
truth attractive, clear, and convincing.

II. FORMS

The literary forms in which Jesus cast his teaching are
almost as interesting as the teaching itself. In fact the
effectiveness of what he said was influenced greatly by
the way he said it. His imagery added spice to his
thought. The variety and beauty of the forms used are
amazing. He was direct and straightforward, making
truth clear and forceful.

1. Concrete Statements

Jesus' teaching was concrete though he was stressing
ideals and principles. He did not philosophize, theorize,
or deal in abstractions. His style is not logical or analyt-
ical but topical and descriptive, and therefore, very impressive. In presenting a new truth he began with things

near at hand and went from them to conclusions. To be
sure, he did give general concepts and principles, but as a
rule he started with percepts and specific instances using
the apperceptive principle. In other words he went from
the known to the unknown, from the concrete to the abstract, from things which appeal to the senses to those
purely in the mental realm. The parables are fine illustrations of the use of this principle. This means that his
teaching was more inductive that deductive. He started
where the people were and took them where he wanted
them to go, which is a very fine procedure in any teaching if one expects to carry a group along with him.

In the Teaching on the Mount he referred to light and
salt, mote and beam, eye and arm, gate and way, grapes
and figs, rock and sand, and other visible objects. He
used birds to teach trust, a little child to demonstrate
humility, a penny to show civic responsibility, an ox in
the ditch to emphasize need, a barren fig tree to stress
fruitfulness, and a cup of cold water to illustrate service.
What could be more effective than to speak of personal
work as "fishing for men," false prophets as "wolves in
sheep's clothing," and Christians as "salt of the earth"
and "light of the world." Even his miracles were concrete. The most effective teachers follow his example
in use of the concrete, using illustrations to make clear
and impress truth if not to convey it. Things that appeal
to the senses catch the imagination, hold the interest, and
are easily remembered. We do well to spend time in securing suitable illustrations for use in our teaching.

2. Pithy Sayings

Jesus' formal, didactic discourse such as the Teaching
on the Mount, is noticeable for its use of short, pithy,
proverbial statements that attract attention, carry truth,
and stick in the memory. They are "condensations of
immemorial experience and worldly wisdom." They are

thus like the maxims of the rabbis who compressed their teaching into such statements as "A good life is better than high birth"; "As is the mother, so is the daughter"; and "He who makes the pleasures of this world his portion, loses those of the world to come." They went home like barbed arrows, "stimulants of our flagging attention, irritants of our prosaic imagination." [1] "The words of the wise are as goads, and as nails fastened by the masters of assemblies" (Eccl. 12: 11).

In this respect his teaching was more nearly like that of the wise men than it was that of the prophets or poets. Says the Dean of Westminster: "If we look back to the older Scriptures for the models on which, in form at least, our Lord's discourses are framed, it is, for the most part, not the Psalms nor the prophecies, nor the historians, but the works of Solomon." [2] These proverbial statements were customary in the East and were prevalent in the atmosphere in which Jesus grew up.

Characteristic of these short, pithy, epigrammatic statements found in the teaching of the Master are such maxims as, "The measure you give will be the measure you get" (Mark 4: 24). Also such proverbial statements as, "One sows and another reaps" (John 4: 37), and "Where your treasure is there will your heart be also" (Matt. 6: 21). Likewise there are those that have been called germ parables such as, "Wherever the body is, there the eagles will be gathered together" (Matt. 24: 28). [3] Another axiomatic saying is: "He who is not with me is against me" (Matt. 12: 30).

Whether these statements were studied or spontaneous we may not know, but they were certainly effective. In our own land in recent years we have seen the forceful-

[1] Curtis, W. A., *Jesus Christ the Teacher,* p. 95, Oxford University Press, 1943.
[2] Quoted by Hinsdale, B. A., in *Jesus as a Teacher,* p. 152, The Christian Publishing Co., St. Louis, 1895.
[3] See McCoy, C. F., *The Art of Jesus as a Teacher,* p. 58, The Judson Press, Philadelphia, 1930.

ness of the pithy sayings of men like Benjamin Franklin, Will Rogers, and J. B. Gambrell. The last named is still more quoted than almost any man among Southern Baptists. We may not be able to coin such statements ourselves for teaching, but we may acquire some of them from others.

3. *Figures of Speech*

Jesus did more than use concrete materials and striking statements. To make his truth more impressive he made frequent use of figures of speech. Horne even went so far as to say that it was more important to feel the beauty of a parable than to understand it. That is rather extreme but it does emphasize their effect on life. In using figures of speech he ran the risk of being misunderstood, but it was worth it in the enlivening effect that it had. The average teacher will not be able to use very many, but where he can, it will add effectiveness to his teaching for they are "like apples of gold in pictures of silver" (Prov. 25: 11). They always add impressiveness.

Parables, of course, constitute the outstanding figure of speech used by Jesus. However, a number of others were used. The simile is common, suggesting likeness as, "How often would I have gathered your children together as a hen gathers her brood under her wings, and you would not!" (Matt. 23: 37). The allegory or sustained comparison is used some as in the teaching, "I am the vine, you are the branches" (John 15: 1-10). The beatitude, a sort of exclamation, is outstanding as, "Oh, the blessedness of the pure in heart, for they shall see God" (Matt. 5: 8, Kent's translation). The hyperbole is an exaggerated statement such as the camel going through the eye of a needle (Matt. 19: 24).

Contrasts are very prominent such as, "Do not lay up for yourselves treasures on earth, but lay up for yourselves treasures in heaven" (Matt. 6: 19-20). The paradox or seeming contradiction is used effectively. "Whosoever would save his life will lose it" (Matt. 16: 25). Sherrill indicates also the use of poetic forms, saying: "Hebrew poetry can be found in the utterances of Jesus, notably parallelism, rhythm, and rhyme." [1] A mastery and use of the various figures of speech will be an invaluable aid to any teacher.

III. Purposes

How did Jesus use the various kinds of materials about which we have been thinking? Were they content materials or merely helps? These questions are live issues in modern teaching, and the example of the Master may give us some light. In general, Weigle is correct, "He went about the work of teaching, not as though he had a certain body of material which he must transmit in a proper, logical, pre-determined order to his pupils, but rather with a clear recognition that these were living, active, needy persons whom he might help to meet wisely the actual circumstances and situations with which they had to do." [2]

1. *To Begin*

Sometimes he started with a statement of Scripture and then elaborated on it as in the Teaching on the Mount when he mentioned what Moses had said about murder, adultery, oaths, vengeance, hate and other matters, and then went on to enlarge upon those teachings and "fulfill" them (Matt. 5: 21-48). For example, he showed that murder consisted in the attitude of heart and not merely the act of killing. Likewise, he stated that adultery was in the lustful look as well as in the

---

[1] *The Rise of Christian Education,* p. 90, The Macmillan Co., New York, 1944.
[2] *Jesus and the Educational Method,* p. 17, The Abingdon Press, New York, 1939.

overt act itself. With due regard for the teachings of the law and the prophets, he went beyond them to give the deeper, inner meaning.

In the light of the reverence in which our pupils hold the Bible, we may well start our teaching with references to it as a means of attracting attention and creating interest. Then we can move on to the applications to life problems. This may be as effective a start as beginning with the problem, and then ending with the Scripture.

Jesus not only used the Scriptures to begin his teaching, but likewise used the experiences of those present as starting points. We have already noted this in the case of the request for a division of the inheritance as a starter for teaching a lesson on covetousness; the murmuring about associating with publicans and sinners as an opportunity for teaching about God's love for the lost; and the complaint about plucking grain on the sabbath as a chance for stressing the true meaning of the sabbath.

Similarly he used the instance of healing the man let down through the roof as an occasion to emphasize his power to forgive sins; and the query as to why he ate with publicans to show that it was not those that were whole but the ones that were sick that needed a physician. These are only a few of the instances that might be given, but they are enough to show that the Master took advantage of occasions to teach truth. In some ways the most striking lessons he taught grew out of situations he confronted in his work, as will often, if not usually, be true with us.

These instances help us to see that the true teacher uses materials as a means and not as an end in teaching. Also, they show that it is better to stick to the pupil rather than to the printed lesson, since in the last analysis we are teaching people rather than lessons. There is no invariable rule as to how to begin a lesson. Whatever

works best is best. One may begin to advantage with
nature, as Jesus did in the parables on the soil, the tares,
the mustard seed, leaven, treasure, and pearls. These
gave him the setting for explaining the kingdom of
heaven (Matt. 13). Many teachers in the elementary
grades do this today.

2. To Clarify

Jesus frequently used scriptural and other materials
to throw light on some statement already made and make
it clearer. This is the meaning of the term illustrate
which literally means to "illuminate" or shine on. He
turned the light of revelation and current incidents on
truths that were not clear that his disciples might see
them. This accounts for the fact that his teaching has
stood out so clearly through the ages. It is at the heart
of the use of parables, where an incident real or imagined
is taken from the natural world or everyday experience
to throw light on some moral or spiritual truth.

In his controversy with the Jews about the sabbath he
referred to the practice of David to illustrate his point
that man is greater than institutions, saying: "He entered the house of God, and ate the bread of the Presence,
which it was not lawful for him to eat, nor for those who
were with him, but only for the priests" (Matt. 12: 4).
On the same occasion and to throw further light on his
statement he says: "Have you not read in the law how
on the sabbath the priests in the temple profane the
sabbath, and are guiltless?" (Matt. 12: 5). An instance
from current events is the reference to the eighteen killed
by the falling of the tower of Siloam, which Jesus used
to impress the need for repentance. References to nature
were made for the same purpose. It was at least partly
for illumination that he quoted from Isaiah in announc-
ing the purpose of his ministry when he stood up in the
synagogue to read.

"Apt illustration's artful aid" is always helpful. It has a tremendous value in all education. The average person will remember a good story much better than he will a general statement of truth or an array of statistics, or even an argument. The vivid illustrations of Charles H. Spurgeon, Billy Sunday, and George W. Truett were probably as telling as the messages themselves. Like barbed arrows they carried their messages home to the listeners. If taken from the Bible, they are more effective still because of general familiarity with it, and high regard for it. There is no finer source for such material than the Old and New Testaments. Every teacher will do well to saturate himself with good illustrations from them as well as from history, biography, fiction, nature, and current events.

3. *To Strengthen*

Along with the Master's use of the Scriptures to introduce a lesson and to make his teaching clear, is his use of them to add emphasis to what he had said. In these instances he used them more as a reference than as a textbook. Just as a speaker or scholar quotes from different sources in his speaking or writing, so Jesus referred to the Scriptures in his teaching. Naturally the testimony of others adds weight to one's statements, provided, of course, those quoted from are recognized. Again it may be said that because of the regard in which it is held, quotations from the Bible are the most effective that can be used. Even lawyers and politicians recognize this and use them in the courtroom and campaigns, that "every word may be confirmed by the evidence of two or three witnesses" (Matt. 18: 16). Herein lies the value of the use of parallel passages.

An instance of this use is his quotation from Isaiah when he was driving the businessmen from the Temple and said, "It is written, 'My house shall be called a house of prayer'; but you make it a den of robbers" (Matt. 21: 13). In concluding the parable on the vineyard and husbandman he quoted: "Have you not read this scripture: 'The very stone which the builders rejected has become the head of the corner'" (Mark 12: 10). When stressing the fact that his coming would bring division as well as peace, he said: "He who believes in me, as the scripture has said, 'Out of his heart shall flow rivers of living water'" (John 7: 38). It was somewhat on this basis that the Master explained to the two on the way to Emmaus the things in the Scriptures regarding himself. In fact there are many instances of his use of the Scriptures to clarify things about himself or his teaching.

Sometimes in a case of stress Jesus went further and appealed to the Scriptures as a final authority or court of last resort. He thus used it somewhat as a lawyer uses a court decision or constitutional law. Of course it was not regarded as something that was arbitrary, but rather as grounded in truth and therefore having the element of finality. A good example of silencing his critics with a reference from the Scriptures is found in his appeal to the testimony of David regarding him as Lord, thus answering the Pharisees' contention that he was David's son (Matt. 22: 41-45).

When he was tempted to cast himself off the Temple and let God support him, he answered: "It is written, 'You shall not tempt the Lord your God'" (Matt. 4: 7; Deut. 6: 16). And when tempted to worship Satan, he said: "It is written, 'You shall worship the Lord your God, and him only shall you serve'" (Matt. 4: 10). Likewise he appealed to the law of Moses as a final authority against the pleas of the Pharisees for liberalizing divorce (Matt. 19: 3-6; Gen. 1: 27; 2: 23-24). Nothing strengthens our teaching more than an appeal "to the law and to the testimony."

TEACHING AIDS

BLACKBOARD OUTLINE

I. Sources

    1. The Scriptures

    2. Natural world

    3. Current affairs

II. Forms

    1. Concrete statements

    2. Pithy sayings

    3. Figures of speech

III. Purposes

    1. To begin

    2. To clarify

    3. To strengthen

TOPICS FOR DISCUSSION

1. How did Jesus acquire his knowledge of the Scriptures?
2. Is it better to work toward or from the Scriptures in teaching?
3. What is the most effective use of the Bible?
4. Why are current events valuable in teaching?
5. Mention other uses that may be made of materials.
6. Give examples of other kinds of figures of speech.

CHAPTER VI

Procedure in a Lesson

JESUS had no fixed procedure in teaching. He was not bound by any routine, or a slave to any system. Rather he was master of them all, and varied his process according to the situation he faced, the objective he had in mind, and the method he followed. He used whatever procedure suited best at the moment. The instance that probably comes nearer than any other to fitting the formal pattern is the teaching of the Samaritan woman at Jacob's well. It has been referred to most frequently and is very familiar. We shall study it as a general illustration of the steps ordinarily involved in presenting a lesson, recognizing that while it has the general essentials, it is suggestive rather than final as a procedure.

I. INTRODUCTION

Obviously every teaching activity must have some sort of beginning. We must start somewhere. It is in some respects the most important part of the procedure. Success or failure may largely depend on the opening sentence, or at least the first few. If attention and interest are not secured then, they may never be. So it is very important to consider carefully the introduction. In fact some teachers spend more time on this part of the lesson than on any other.

1. *What It Means*

The introduction or beginning of a lesson is the attracting of attention and directing it toward the topic for the day. As the police announcer is "calling all cars" so the teacher is "calling all minds." Until that has been done no learning takes place. One cannot teach either without or against the attention. It is like pulling a car without its motor running, or pulling it with the gear in reverse. Or to vary the figure it is like an engine running without the coaches attached. Until the teacher has secured the attention of the class there is no need to try to go any further. He had just as well back up and start over. The important thing in the introduction is securing the attention of the pupil, so that his mind may be connected up with the lesson to be taught.

To secure attention some sort of contact must be made with the pupil's mind. One must get over into the area where the pupil is. In other words he must connect up with his thinking in some way. Edward Leigh Pell well says: "The difference between a trained teacher and a novice is never more apparent than in the first five minutes of the lesson hour. The novice looks first at the lesson. The trained teacher looks first at the pupils."[1]

In other words he seeks to find out what the pupil is thinking about and start with that. As Patterson DuBois has put it: "The mind is a castle that can be taken neither by stealth nor by storm. But there is a natural way of approach and a gate of easy entry—an experience or point of contact with life."[2] There teacher and pupil meet on common ground.

At this point it might be well to say that claptrap methods of securing attention are of little value. Calling for it, pounding on the desk, and doing something sensational may get the attention of the class away from other things, but they do not necessarily turn it to the lesson in hand. They are short-lived and may be even distracting. Stories that are not in line with the thought

---

[1] *Secrets of Sunday School Teaching*, p. 73, Fleming H. Revell Co., New York, 1912.
[2] *The Point of Contact in Teaching*, p. 5, Dodd, Mead, and Co., New York, 1913.

may carry the mind on a wild-goose chase as easily as they start it on the lesson trail. Likewise, the teacher should be careful about getting off on interesting but irrelevant topics such as airplanes, football, fashions, and politics in order to attract attention. It is not always easy to pull a diverted car back on the main road.

The best point of contact or beachhead for securing attention is the natural interest of the pupil, or something interesting in the lesson itself to which the mind can be directed. Curiosity or the desire to know is central. When that is aroused the pupil will be started on the main line. Of course the teacher's interest in the subject counts for a lot. Weigle well says: "We fail unless we get the pupil interested in the lesson itself. Our problem is not to make a lesson interesting by trick of method or by adding to it stories or other material pleasant but extraneous; it is to bring out of each lesson its intrinsic interest."[1] One may start with an inner interest, or a problem related to it, and go from that to something in the lesson that bears on it.

All of this means that we must start from, or tie up with, innate desires or needs, for one "cannot stand off at a distance and throw knowledge at a pupil." And the pupil's needs grow out of the native instincts. One of them is the drive for self-preservation and security, here and hereafter. Another is the urge for mating and the propagation of the race. The craving for power and control is likewise a very strong urge. Outstanding also is the yearning for social fellowship and recognition. Out of these are the issues of life. They are centers around which most of life revolves. Interest will be aroused and attention held as the teacher connects up with them.

In order to tie in effectively with instinctive desires we must know as much as possible about the lives of our

[1] *The Teacher*, p. 124, American Baptist Publication Society, Philadelphia, 1917.

pupils—their interests, experiences, hobbies, and problems. One ought to know something about the home life, the public school studies and experiences, the professional activities and problems, the social and recreational life, and the religious and moral problems. He should study the individual from books, observation, and personal testimony. Then he can start with interests and lead up to the Sunday school lesson, or begin with the lesson in the light of these situations and bring out principles bearing on them. In either case he will have a point of contact.

2. *An Instance from Jesus*

The Master was effective in getting the point of contact. Whether he was dealing with his friends or his enemies he connected up with their minds. Probably the most striking example is the instance of the discussion with the woman at Jacob's well (John 4: 1-7). The teaching situation was difficult. Almost every conceivable obstacle stood in the way. According to the Jewish system of reckoning, it was about the noon hour, on a warm day, after the Master had walked quite a distance. He was tired, hot, dirty, thirsty and hungry, and in a poor physical condition for an interview. The woman had come for a pail of water, and was likely hot and hurried, and not ready to be taught. They had also the disadvantage of being strangers. They were poles apart as to righteousness, he being sinless and she debased. He was a man and she a woman, which was a barrier in Oriental lands. He was a Jew and she a Samaritan, and the two peoples were highly prejudiced against each other. In discussing the incident B. W. Spilman says: "There was about as much love between a Samaritan and a Jew as between a fox terrier and a strange cat." [1]

[1] *A Study in Religious Pedagogy*, p. 34, Fleming H. Revell Co., New York, 1920.

So the odds were all against a favorable point of contact. Yet he broke through all of these barriers with the simplest, most humanitarian, least antagonistic and most nearly natural introduction that could be made—a request for a drink of water. A hurried, prejudiced, sinful stranger even of the opposite sex could not resent that. Probably the most striking part of the famous painting of the Battle of Atlanta in the Cyclorama there, is that of a soldier sharing his canteen of water with a wounded enemy. This request of Jesus avoided all issues, got a favorable response and was a master stroke. After getting a contact and the attention, it was easy to make the transition from natural to "living" water, and then he was out in the open and headed straight for the goal.

All through his ministry we find similar instances of beginnings. In practically every case he appealed to the thing uppermost in mind, such as occupation, problems and needs. In the Teaching on the Mount he congratulated those that hungered, mourned, and were poor, assuring them of the richer blessings in store for them (Matt. 5: 3-9). On the last day of the feast he called out to the parched multitudes, "If any one thirst, let him come to me and drink" (John 7: 37). Frequently he referred to the teachings of Moses, which they revered greatly, as a point of departure for teaching his own truths. When the scribes and Pharisees criticized, he took their attitude as a starting point. He attended social functions, and ate and drank with publicans and sinners to secure a closer relation. Even a miracle was used to pave the way for presenting a truth. It is likely that the multitudes followed him largely because of vital contacts previously made.

Whatever the teaching method employed, his first task was to get a point of contact—arouse interest and attract attention. It might be by means of a request, an object, a question, a statement, or a story. Whatever procedure was necessary to do this, he followed. Of course knowing what was in man's mind, he could do it more effectively than we can hope to do. But in any case it is with us, as it was with him, the first task, and until accomplished, our most important one.

II. DEVELOPMENT

Having turned the pupil's mind toward the lesson for the day, the big job is still ahead. This is true both as to holding interest and attention, and presenting the truth. One must go on to state, clarify, and clinch the lesson. The truth must be brought out, thought through, realized keenly, and the underlying principles and implications grasped. The minds must be held to the problem until the job has been finished.

1. *Essentials in It*

Basal to the whole task of effective lesson presentation is an understanding of the fundamental laws of learning. These have been well stated as the laws of readiness, exercise, and effect. The first, as already mentioned, means that when a person is ripe for an experience, to have it is satisfying, to avoid it is annoying; so materials that are appropriate must be used. The second suggests that everything else being equal, the more we do a thing, the more likely it is to become a part of us. It is the old emphasis on repetition and habit. And the third states that when the effect of an experience is satisfying, we tend to repeat it; and when annoying, to avoid it. Therefore our teaching must meet the needs of life.

These principles should guide in planning and presenting a lesson. Also we should keep in mind the difference between transmissive and creative teaching; the former consisting of passing on to another our ideas without any particular thought on his part, and the latter is helping him to discover the truth for himself. One method develops followers, and the other leaders.

Before undertaking to present a lesson it should be carefully planned. This is as essential as seeking to find out the meaning of the Scripture material used. And in planning, the first thing is to select the main truth to be taught. This means that having studied the setting, facts, and truths of the passage, we will select one or more truths that we think the class should have. If the material will admit of it, it is often better for the sake of emphasis to have just one, as in the case of teaching the rich young ruler; though there will be many cases where several truths are involved, as in the Beatitudes.

Having a definite plan makes our teaching specific and to the point. It gives clear-cut aims. This unit of teaching of course should fit in with the larger aims for the quarter, and for the whole series of lessons. And again it should be said that to select each Sunday the truth the class needs most will necessitate an understanding of the times in which we live, and of the personal life of each member of the class. This is necessary if we are to teach people rather than lessons.

Then comes the matter of presenting the lesson in such an interesting manner as to carry the class along with the teacher, and make the truth vivid and impressive. This is easier said than done, but it is very necessary. It involves a clear understanding of the material on the part of the teacher, and a genuine interest in the pupils and the issues involved. When one teaches as if it does not make any difference, then it does not make any difference whether or not he teaches.

Sunday school teaching is more than helping the pupil acquire knowledge. Proper presentation involves the development of attitudes, and the introduction of control into conduct. It necessitates keeping alert to the ideas and attitudes of the class and using them as much as possible. This means the use of illustrations, questions, and discussions frequently. It likewise calls for visual aids, dramatic activities, and project procedures. Methods of course will vary according to the age of the pupil, the kind of material, and the ability of the teacher. Whatever works best is best.

It is exceedingly important that the teacher stick to the main theme and not allow himself to be sidetracked by irrelevant matters. This is not easy to do, but it is important. It does not mean of course that he will ignore relevant questions that are not in the schedule, for these may be more important than the material itself, but it does mean that he will not allow the pupils consciously or unconsciously to lead him away from the main line. He will stick to the pupil and the main theme, if not to the exact materials. He will need to guard carefully his time, so as to omit nothing essential, give each part its due emphasis, and not to rush. He is to guide and direct a learning process as well as to impart interesting and valuable information.

2. *An Example from Jesus*

The Teacher did the things mentioned in developing his theme with the Samaritan woman (John 4: 7-26). Having introduced the natural and desirable subject of "water" and been faced with the sidetracking rebuff that a Jew should not make such a request of a Samaritan, he told her if she understood him she would ask him for "living water." Still she did not understand, objected that the well was deep, that he had nothing with which to draw, and sought to argue by saying he was not greater than Jacob who provided the well. But he stuck to his topic of water, and said that the kind he would give, would quench thirst permanently, and become "a spring of water welling up to eternal life" (v. 14). Now he was at the heart of his subject and had her curiosity and interest, though still she did not under-

stand what he meant, for she requested this water so as
not to thirst, or have to return to the well to draw again.

In order to make clear his idea, to emphasize the spiritual, and to deepen conviction, he told her to go and
call her husband. She said she had none. He answered
that this was true for she had had five, and the one she
lived with now was not her husband. Seeing that he was
a prophet and getting close to her life, she tried to
divert the discussion by raising the Samaritan-Jewish
dispute as to whether worship should be in her mountain
or in his Jerusalem. He refused to be diverted, and came
back with the statement that true worship does not
involve a place but an attitude, "in spirit and truth,"
for God is spirit. When she stated that the coming Messiah would clear up all these things, he answered, "I who
speak to you am he" (v. 26). Thus he attracted her attention, kept her interest, refused to be sidetracked, and
clarified and clinched the truth. It is a splendid demonstration of the development of a lesson, and we will do
well to study it frequently as a matchless example.

Other instances of Jesus' development of a lesson could
be given. While this case involved the discussion method,
some were by lecture such as the Teaching on the Mount,
others by the use of story as in the fifteenth chapter of
Luke, and still others made use of objects such as putting
the child in the midst. Likewise, demonstrations were
used, as when he answered the doubt of John the Baptist
through showing what he was doing; questions were employed as when he asked the origin of baptism; and even
the dramatic method, as in baptism and the Lord's Supper. The Master did not stop until he had made clear
and convincing his teaching.

III. Conclusion

The final stage in the teaching procedure is that of
coming to a conclusion or an application. With some it

is about the most difficult part of the task. This seems
to be true with teachers as well as preachers. Often very
little attention is paid to it, hoping all will come out
well. But it is too important to be neglected, for it is
likely that what is said last will be most impressive and
longest remembered.

1. *What Is Involved*

It is very evident that a teaching procedure has not
been finished when only the facts of the scriptural lesson
have been presented. This may leave the pupil's mind
wandering around in a distant land 2000 years ago,
as happened with a group of adults in a lesson dealing with the healing activities of Christ on a sabbath
day. The truth needs to be brought down to date and
applied to present-day problems and to the persons in
the class, if it admits of an application. And it needs to
be made emphatic. Sometimes if the study is on historical facts or a number of truths, a good summarizing
at the close will be effective, both to get all of the teaching before the class and to give emphasis by way of
repetition. The nature of the lesson and the needs of
the class will determine the kind of conclusion to be
reached. The method used will determine largely the
particular form of closing.

It is very important to deduce from the facts and
specific truths of the Scripture that is studied the fundamental, underlying principle involved. Otherwise, we get
unorganized facts or truths and do not see the basal
principle. Hence we are unable to apply it to the present day. The big thing about any lesson is the underlying truth. For example, the study on a sabbath day's
healing, previously referred to, should have stressed not
only Jesus' specific activities but also his underlying
interest in the wholeness of life and the fundamental
purpose of his ministry to serve those who needed a

physician rather than the ones who were already whole. In the case of the rich young ruler the emphasis was to put Christ above material interests.

Also an application of the principle to life today should be stressed. To do this one needs to think in terms of the community in which he lives, or the world as a whole. This may be from the standpoint of the church or of the social order. To carry the lesson on healing to its proper conclusion, the teacher should have stressed the place of the Red Cross, hospitals, nurses, and doctors in society today in relieving human suffering. Furthermore, as far as possible the application should be made to the personal lives of those present. Otherwise the teaching has not been properly related to life. In the lesson mentioned on healing, one should go on to show our responsibility to give money to provide hospitals, doctors, and nurses for the sick, or to render personal assistance. Our lesson should come down to earth.

In the conclusion good illustrations are very effective both in making truth vivid and in deepening impressions regarding it. Nothing inspires more than seeing truth incarnate. No argument can be as effective in securing funds for an orphanage as the story of some waif that has been redeemed by it. The same is true of hospitals and healing. Statistics or eloquence cannot go as far in getting funds for foreign missions as the recounting of the services of a Judson or of a Livingstone. The same applies to drives for war needs and suffering humanity. So it is usually helpful to climax the conclusion of a lesson with a good illustration, both to clarify the truth and to arouse to action. This largely accounts for Jesus' extensive use of parables.

2. *The Practice of Jesus*

Since the disciples returned just as the Master was stating to the Samaritan woman that he was the expected Messiah, no formal conclusion or application seems to have been made. Even so he had reached the climax of his teaching. And, in effect, there was a fine closing, for we learn that she left her water pot, forgetting to get what she had gone after, and went into the city testifying about him. So evidently he had led her up to the proper conclusion not only intellectually but also in attitude and in response, which are the final tests of a conclusion. A formal conclusion may not be necessary.

In the case of the inquiring lawyer he did make a very practical and definite application. Having emphasized the necessity of loving one's neighbor as himself and having given the story of the Good Samaritan to illustrate neighborliness, he asked the lawyer which of the three who came along the road proved to be a neighbor to the injured man. And when the lawyer replied that it was the man who showed mercy, Jesus said: "Go and do likewise" (Luke 10: 37). He not only came to the point of the lesson, but applied it to the man, being personal as well as specific. He did not leave a pupil in mid-air when he taught him.

A somewhat similar application was made in the instance of the Master's dealing with the rich young ruler. After he had stated to him certain of the Ten Commandments, found out the young man's place of weakness, and diagnosed his need, he said: "You lack one thing; go, sell all that you have, and give it to the poor, . . . and come, follow me" (Mark 10: 21). It was a very definite and specific application, fitted to the needs of the young man. And turning to the crowd he gave further emphasis by saying: "How hard it will be for those who have riches to enter the kingdom of God!" (Mark 10: 23). The Master Teacher always arrived at the point.

In concluding this chapter on procedure, it seems appropriate to say a few words about checking results, for in a sense this is a part of the teaching activity. Several types of tests have been used. One is the old-fashioned question and answer method. Another is the multiple choice in which the pupil selects from two or more answers the proper one. Another is checking, as true or false, statements based on the lesson. Still another is completing or filling in an omitted part of a Scripture or other statement. Occasionally tests are made of attitudes as well as of knowledge. Observing personally and checking with parents and public school teachers will help to get at results.

While Jesus seems not to have made much use of tests, he did seek in various ways to find out something of the results of his teaching. On one occasion he asked his disciples, "Who do you say that I am?" (Matt. 16: 15). He was seeking to find out how far their understanding had progressed. Also he said on another occasion, "You will know them by their fruits" (Matt. 7: 16). Evidently he observed outcomes in order to check the results of his work. And we know that he got a report on the work of the seventy when they returned from a missionary tour (Luke 10: 17). Also he mentions signs or fruits as tests of the genuineness of believers. We too should check results if we are to know whether or not our teaching is getting over into life.

TEACHING AIDS

I. Introduction
  1. What it means
  2. An instance from Jesus

II. Development
  1. Essentials in it
  2. An example from Jesus

III. Conclusion
  1. What is involved
  2. The practice of Jesus

TOPICS FOR DISCUSSION

1. Mention other interests than those stated.
2. Explain Jesus' strategy with the Samaritan woman.
3. How do you develop your lessons?
4. Mention other lesson developments by Jesus.
5. State the most helpful closing for a lesson.
6. What is the best method for checking results?

CHAPTER VII

Some Methods He Used

WHETHER OR NOT the Master consciously studied or used methods in his teaching is questionable. The likelihood is that he did not, especially in the sense in which we do. That he was a master in the use of methods, however, is evident from the skilful way he used them in his work. They were probably natural to him rather than being deliberately studied and planned, and grew out of the occasion and need. However, the result is essentially the same. He was matchless in the use of methods and taught as never man taught. Practically all of those common in teaching today were used at least in embryo. We shall notice some of them briefly in this discussion.

I. OBJECTS

While not outstanding in his activity, Jesus did teach by means of object lessons. He sought to make truth concrete and vivid, and this method naturally fitted in. He utilized the general principle in one way or another more than the specific practice. But there are some definite instances of the use of objects that are very interesting.

1. *Nature and Value*

Ordinarily we think of object lessons as the use of things that symbolize or suggest the truth to be taught. They include models, pictures, drawings, maps, and similar materials. A model of Noah's ark, or of the tabernacle, or of a foreign mission compound is very helpful in making clear and vivid the scene to be discussed. The use of good pictures or blackboard drawings will also help in presenting biblical and missionary scenes and other truths. A planetarium in a public school showing the relative positions of the sun and earth made the reason for the change of seasons much more clear than the abstract definition which said it is due to "the inclination of the earth's axis toward the plane of the ecliptic together with its revolution around the sun." However, symbolic objects such as a loaf of bread to represent Christ as the Bread of Life, or clarifying cloudy water by means of chemicals to show how regeneration cleanses the heart are questionable, for children may mistake the figure for the reality.

The value of the object grows out of its appeal to the eye and the definiteness with which it represents the thing portrayed. The eye gate is practically always a more effective avenue of approach to the pupil's mind than the ear gate, some claiming that more than 80 per cent of our knowledge comes that way. Almost invariably we remember what we see better than what we hear. One of the poorest teachers the writer ever knew taught one of the most effective lessons he ever received, by drawing on the blackboard a picture of a ladder wider at the top than at the bottom, to illustrate the fact that the higher one climbs in the realm of education, the greater are his opportunities in life. Teachers do well to seek skill in the use of the blackboard.

Edward Leigh Pell says: "We talk of principles in general when we ought to show things in the concrete. Many a teacher spends half an hour trying to explain a thing by word of mouth when a pencil and a slip of paper and two or three crooked marks would make it clear as daylight in two minutes." And he adds, "If the Catholic is more devoted to his church than the Protestant, it is largely because of what the Catholic is made to see and handle while the Protestant is left to work it out with his imagination." [1]

2. Uses by Jesus

One of the most outstanding instances of the use of object lessons by the Master was the one of putting the child in the midst to teach the attitude one should have toward the kingdom (Matt. 18: 1-4). The disciples were thinking of it as something with gradation and rank, and therefore with promotion and recognition. Self-seeking ambition was getting the upper hand and they were questioning among themselves as to who would be pre-eminent. Hence the question propounded to Christ: "Who is the greatest in the kingdom of heaven?" (v. 1). Apparently without any explanation or discussion he called a child and placed it before them. As they saw modesty, unselfishness, and humility exemplified in it, he told them that they must become in attitude like little children in order to get into the kingdom at all. Then he added, "Whoever humbles himself like this child, he is the greatest in the kingdom of heaven" (v. 4). It was humanity's greatest lesson on the evil of pride and the value of self-effacement.

Similarly we have the instance of Jesus washing the disciples' feet (John 13: 1-15). It was the custom in Oriental lands to wear sandals. Naturally as people traveled over dirt roads their feet became soiled. Consequently on entering a home for a visit or a feast it was customary for the servant to take a basin of water and a towel, and bathe and dry the visitor's feet. In this case there was apparently none present, so the Master assumed the role of a menial servant and washed and wiped the disciples' feet. He did it in a normal and natural fashion to meet a need. In doing so he showed

---

[1] *Secrets of Sunday School Teaching,* p. 93, Fleming H. Revell Co., New York, 1912.

the dignity and greatness of humble service. It was a demonstration of what anyone should do under similar circumstances. It was another object lesson on humility and one of the most impressive teachings he ever gave. He closed it by saying: "If I then, your Lord and Teacher, have washed your feet, you also ought to wash one another's feet. For I have given you an example, that you also should do as I have done to you" (vv. 14-15).

On another occasion representatives of the Pharisees and Herodians came trying him with the query as to the lawfulness of giving tribute to Caesar. Without waiting to argue he asked for a piece of tribute money, and they handed him a penny. Holding the object before them he said: "Whose likeness and inscription is this? They said, 'Caesar's.' Then he said to them, 'Render therefore to Caesar the things that are Caesar's, and to God the things that are God's'" (Matt. 22: 15-22). He did at least two things in this use of an object. For one thing he attracted attention, since one could not fail to get it by such a method. Then he used it as a means of teaching the responsibility of taxpaying, since it was to Caesar, and also our obligation to give to the Lord, since what we have is his. Probably no statement he made has been more widely quoted.

Other instances include his instruction to the twelve to shake the dust off their feet in a symbolical fashion when in their missionary work they left a house or city that did not receive them kindly (Matt. 10: 14). It showed that they had discharged their duty to the community and no longer owed a responsibility. Also his healing of the palsied man, brought by four friends, furnished an objective demonstration of his power to forgive a man's sins when the scribes accused him of blasphemy and claimed only God could forgive (Mark 2: 6-12). If he could heal palsy, he could forgive sins, for the

latter was not more difficult than the former. And still
another was his demonstration of his deity through the
healing of the blind, deaf, lame, and others when John the
Baptist in a state of doubt sent messengers to inquire if
he were really the Christ (Matt. 11: 2-6).

So we have abundant evidence of Christ's use of object lessons to make his teaching attractive, clear, and
impressive. Some of his best remembered teachings were
thus presented. We can use the same method if we will.
C. H. Woolston served as pastor of the East Baptist
Church in Philadelphia for more than forty years, largely
because he centered his ministry on children, and developed an elaborate system of object lessons in presenting his messages. We can use the blackboard,
posters, and reproductions of great paintings to advantage.

II. DRAMATICS

Christ made use of the dramatic method quite a bit
in his teaching either in a formal or informal fashion.
And religious workers have come to do so in an in-
creasing manner in recent years. A number of books
have been written in the field and some churches are
even providing special equipment and leadership for
this purpose. It is definitely an educational procedure.

1. *Meaning and Scope*

Dramatizing carries the idea of re-enacting a scene.
We think of it as the reproduction of a historical event
or the portrayal of a current activity. In other words
it is the effort to portray in as nearly as possible in a
natural setting some situation in history or modern life.
It is, therefore, primarily an imitative and reproductive
activity. However, the term is used more broadly to
cover the presenting of truth as well as the reproduction of facts. So we may think of it as the acting out of

a truth or lesson whether or not there is any definite
basis of fact. Dramatic activities may include biblical
incidents, missionary activities, temperance lessons,
and other events to be presented and lessons to be
taught. An element of the dramatic may enter into
any teaching.

This method has distinct values both for the participants and for the other members of the class. The par-
ticipant has to study his part carefully and put himself
in the place of his character. Thought, imagination,
feeling, and will are brought into play. Sympathies and
interests are stimulated. The principle of learning by
doing is utilized, which is more effective than merely re-
citing a lesson or listening to a lecture. "Playing like" is
a valuable way of learning. Likewise the observer learns
more readily than through the recitation or lecture
methods. Since dramatic activities utilize the eye as
well as the ear, and bring in garb and color as well as
movement, they are a most effective means of presenting
truth. The play spirit appeals to all ages. "It almost
runs the legs off the growing youngsters. It is the jolly
good companion during college days. It even forgets
to respect gray hairs and creaking joints." [1]

Teaching through dramatics may be done in various
ways. It may be done formally with plans made ahead,
as when a class presented the good Samaritan. Or it
may be informal with the teacher assigning parts after
getting into the class and having the lesson dramatized,
as the writer once witnessed a class in reading in a
Catholic parish school. It may be the prepared play,
the shadow play, tableau, or pantomime. Puppets, "little jets" and clothespins may be brought into use. A
very effective portrayal of the story of the good Samaritan can be done with puppets. It may be in the class or

---

[1] Meredith, William V., *Pageantry and Dramatics in Religious
Education,* The Abingdon Press, New York, 1921.

in the department program. The writer can never forget the dramatizing of a Sunday school lesson on it by Juniors in the department assembly. The teacher himself may present a lesson dramatically, as Billy Sunday often did in his preaching. History, biography, missionary activities, moral and social conditions, and other lessons may be given in dramatic form. Interest will be created, attention secured, information acquired, and experiences deepened.

2. *Emphasis by Jesus*

The Master was in good company when he utilized the dramatic method in teaching. The Jews before him had done such. The festivals were especially dramatic, as the people, in observing the Feast of the Passover, re-enacted the scenes connected with the sparing of the first-born in Egypt. Also they dramatized in the Feast of Tabernacles the experiences of dwelling in booths as they had on the journey out of Egypt. The ceremonials of the tabernacle and Temple were dramatic, especially those connected with the purifying of the worshipers and the selecting, slaying, and offering of animals in connection with the various sacrifices. Even the curtains and the arrangements of these institutions had special significance. Also the prophets were rather dramatic, as when Isaiah went barefooted about the streets of Jerusalem showing the people the poverty that lay ahead; when Jeremiah wore a wooden yoke about his neck to warn them of the coming captivity; and when Ezekiel made a model of Jerusalem and dramatically laid siege to it.

Jesus did not give formal dramatic programs but utilized the principle. Probably the outstanding use of the dramatic method by him was in the inauguration of baptism and the Lord's Supper. They are the New Testament successors of the Old Testament feasts. They are not mere commands, or ceremonials, or fellowship activities, but rather teaching procedures. In dramatic form they re-enact the most significant experiences and teachings in the life of Christ. The Lord's Supper portrays his broken body and shed blood for the redemption of humanity, and our participation in the benefits of this experience as we accept him. Baptism pictures Christ's resurrection from the dead (the sign he promised of his being the Son of God), our death to sin and resurrection to "walk in newness of life" (the greatest single human experience), and the final resurrection of the dead (the hope of immortality). These are the essentials of Christianity. As J. F. Love has said: "With the voice men preach the gospel to the ear, with the ordinances they preach it to the eye." [1]

This conception lifts these activities from the low plane of empty ceremonials to the high level of the most effective didactic procedure known to man—that of seeing truth re-enacted rather than merely reading about it, or hearing it stated. It gives new values to old practices, and justifies the stand of Baptists through the ages on these memorial observances. We are not "old fogies," but up-to-date pedagogues. Modern educational methods have justified our stand. So the participants can count it an honor to have the privilege of thus proclaiming to the world in the most impressive manner the essentials of the gospel. This conception takes away the idea that the Lord's Supper is a fellowship affair, and forever answers the age-long discussion as to the subject and mode of baptism. And it is probably the strongest argument against "alien immersion," for if one's immersion has taken place in an atmosphere which precludes its proclaiming the truth intended, it has lost its meaning.

[1] Love and Gambrell, *The Gospel for the Eye,* p. 12, The Baptist Standard Publishing Co., Dallas, 1911.

Among the other dramatic activities which characterized the Teacher's ministry was his driving the money
changers from the Temple (Matt. 21: 12-16). He found
that the Jews were abusing the privilege of selling animals and fowls for sacrifices to those who did not have
them, and were making it a money-making proposition
rather than a means of service. So he took a scourge
of cords, drove them out, scattered their fowls and animals, and poured out their money, saying: "'My house
shall be called a house of prayer'; but you make it a
den of robbers" (v. 13). Thus he showed dramatically
the sacredness of the Temple and of worship. "The
cleansing of the temple was not done for its own sake so
much as to teach men one more great lesson on reverence." [1]

Also in dramatic fashion the Master rode triumphantly
into Jerusalem amid the waving of branches and the
applause of the multitudes. It was after the manner of
a conquering hero coming home, except that he was on
a donkey rather than in a chariot, escorted by worshipers instead of soldiers, and demonstrated spiritual
kingship rather than political rule (Matt. 21: 7-11). It
was a striking, dramatic act, one of the most impressive
in his entire ministry. So in various ways Jesus utilized
the dramatic method in his teaching.

III. Stories

Undoubtedly the distinctive method used by the Master was the parable or story. It stands out more prominently in his teaching than any other. So noticeable is
it that we think of it as almost characteristic of him as
a teacher, and we remember his stories above everything
else. He was unquestionably the world's greatest story-
teller.

[1] Hitchcock, A. W., *The Psychology of Jesus,* p. 187, The Pilgrim
Press, Boston, 1907.

1. *Importance and Uses*

The word "parable" literally means "thrown along-side." It is a story or illustration taken from a familiar phase of life to throw light on one not so familiar. It is a vivid presentation of truth. William Sanday says: "They are scenes, or short stories, taken from nature or from common life, which present some leading thought or principle capable of being transformed to the higher spiritual life of man." [1] H. H. Horne adds: "A parable is a comparison between familiar facts and spiritual truths." [2] As a teaching method it is practically identical with the story, though some are so short as to be more of the nature of comparisons than stories. These have been characterized as germ parables.

The story method is especially valuable in teaching. It is concrete, appeals to the imagination, has a free and easy style, and is interesting and effective. It is a method which "in unapproachable beauty and finish, stands unrivalled in the annals of human speech." People who turn away from facts and arguments will listen readily to stories. Not only that, but they will remember them and be influenced by them. Seminary students who would not come to hear a prominent man in a lecture series, attend in crowds at an off-hour to hear him tell stories. They are applicable to children and grown-ups alike. Though he has been dead for years, there is rarely a meeting anywhere among Southern Baptists where some story related by J. B. Gambrell is not told. *Uncle Tom's Cabin* had much to do with freeing the slaves. Novels "influence conduct more than books on ethics." "Let me tell the stories," says G. Stan-

---

[1] Hastings *Dictionary of the Bible,* Vol. 2, p. 17, Charles Scribner's Sons, New York, 1916.
[2] *Jesus the Master Teacher,* p. 77, The Association Press, New York, 1920.

ley Hall, "and I care not who writes the textbooks."[1]

There are three ways in which the story may be used in teaching. One of them is to secure the attention. This is the practice of the newspaper reporter. He starts with the most striking part of his account and works back to detailed facts. It is likewise practiced by the speaker and the teacher. Margaret Slattery almost invariably began an address or a book with some striking story. Another way is to use the story to throw light on some principle or abstract truth that has already been stated. Preachers and other speakers make large use of stories or illustrations to make clearer the "three points" in the sermon or address. It is especially valuable in the application of truth. And a third way to use the story is to utilize it to present the entire lesson. This characterized the fable, and is the way by which lessons are frequently presented today, especially to children. It has the added value of letting the pupil draw his own conclusion.

2. Examples from Jesus

It is interesting to notice the Master Teacher's large use of stories or parables in his teaching. In fact they have been called "the consummation of his art." About one fourth of his words as recorded by Mark and about one half as recorded by Luke are in the form of parables. The term "parable" is used about fifty times in the New Testament. If one includes under this head the maxims or germ parables, the allegory, and other illustrations, probably a hundred can be found. They deal with persons, animals, plants, and inanimate life. Horne lists a total of sixty-one, thirty-four of which deal with persons, such as the good Samaritan; four with animals, such as the lost sheep; seven with plants, as

[1] Quoted by E. P. St. John in *Stories and Story Telling,* p. 6, The Pilgrim Press, Boston, 1910.

the mustard seed, and sixteen with things, as the four soils. If the parables were eliminated from Jesus' teaching, much of it would be gone. And if he had not used the method he would not have been anything like so effective.

An instance of beginning with a story or parable is that of telling about the four kinds of soils and the response they made to the seed sown (Matt. 13: 1-9). He presents a picture of a man sowing seed, some of which fell along the road on the hard, impenetrable ground and the birds devoured them. Others fell among the rocks where the soil was thin, warmed quickly and the seed sprouted but had no roots to support them. Others fell among thorns and were choked out by their dense growth. And some fell on good soil, took root and produced thirty to a hundredfold. That was all he said then except to give a warning about hearing.

Later when the disciples requested it, he gave his teachings based on the parable. The roadside soil represents the preoccupied or inattentive hearer from whom the truth bounds like hail off a roof. The rocky soil pictures the superficial or emotional person who responds readily without depth of conviction, but gives up when the going is hard. The soil among thorns portrays the preoccupied individual who lets work and pleasure prevent fruit bearing. And the good soil represents those who listened, received the truth wholeheartedly and acted on it. No one could ever forget that story or its meaning.

A good illustration of the use of the story to throw light on truth previously stated is the parable of the good Samaritan (Luke 10: 25-37). A tantalizing lawyer asked what to do to have eternal life, and answered his own question by quoting the commandment on loving God with the whole heart, mind, strength, and soul, and one's neighbor as himself. Then he raised the self-defense question, "Who is my neighbor?" (v. 29). Jesus

presented no finespun argument or theory. Rather he
proceeded to make the truth clear by telling the story of
the man en route from Jerusalem to Jericho who was
beaten, robbed, and left half dead. After both a priest
and a Levite, (both of whom professionally should have
been interested) had passed by on the other side, a
Samaritan (whose national prejudices might have ex-
cused him), came to his aid, bound up his wounds, took
him to a hotel, and provided money for care and treatment. Deftly the Saviour asked: "Which of these three
. . . proved neighbor to the man . . .?" (v. 36), (rather
than to whom was he a neighbor). The lawyer could
only answer that it was the man who helped. It was
an unanswerable argument against the lawyer's lack of
neighborliness.

The finest example of teaching an entire lesson by
means of stories is found in the fifteenth chapter of
Luke. When the Pharisees and scribes complained because Jesus was being too hospitable to the publicans
(tax collectors) and sinners (vile people), he answered
their murmurings not with arguments or censure but
with three stories—"The Lost Coin," "The Lost Sheep,"
and "The Lost Son." All were something of value, out
of pocket, and the occasion of distress. (So were these
publicans and sinners of worth, lost, and should be the
objects of concern to the scribes and Pharisees.) All
were diligently sought, found, and the object of great
rejoicing. (So should these down-and-out people be
sought after, received and rejoiced over rather than
scorned as they were by these teachers.) It was a beautiful and telling picture of God's rejoicing over the sinner that repents, in contrast with the disdainful attitude
of these supposedly religious leaders. No further explanation or argument was needed. With the Master's
art the mirror of divine truth was held before these
heartless critics, and their sinful attitude laid bare.

He was indeed a Master in the use of object lessons, dramatic methods, and stories or parables in his teaching. It was the use of these along with his marvelous personality that had much to do in attracting the multitudes to him, and causing his truths to be remembered and repeated through the centuries. We will do well to study ways and means of using them in our teaching. Visual, dramatic, and illustrative aids are here to stay.

TEACHING AIDS

BLACKBOARD OUTLINE

I. Objects
   1. Nature and value
   2. Uses by Jesus

II. Dramatics
   1. Meaning and scope
   2. Emphasis by Jesus

III. Stories
   1. Importance and uses
   2. Examples from Jesus

TOPICS FOR DISCUSSION

1. What is the danger in the use of objects?
2. Mention Jesus' most striking object lesson.
3. Differentiate dramatics and object lessons.
4. Evaluate baptism as a teaching activity.
5. Explain the meaning of the term "parable."
6. Which was Jesus' greatest story? Why?

CHAPTER VIII

Other Methods He Employed

JESUS did not limit himself to any one method of teaching. Nor did he magnify one method above another, except that he seems to have used the parable or story more frequently than any other. If he thought of methods at all he evidently considered all of them legitimate and felt that which ever works best under the circumstances is best.

The age group to be taught, the kind of lesson to be used, and the inclination of the teacher will likely be the determining factors in the selection of methods at any time. In all probability we shall use some of all methods in most of our teaching, or at least shift from one to another.

I. LECTURES

The lecture method is the use of discourse in the presentation of a lesson by a teacher to a class. The teacher does all, or practically all, of the talking. It is supposed to be a systematic, comprehensive presentation but may not be. It may include the use of the blackboard or other materials, or may not. Woodrow Wilson once spoke of it as "the literary method in the classroom." It has also been characterized as "didactic discourse."

1. *Strength and Weaknesses*

Probably no teaching method has been more widely used and generally criticized than this one. The irony of the situation is for people to lecture against the use of the lecture. It has both its strong and weak points and we should judge it on its merits. There are several values in its use. It is very helpful when one has a class so large that he can use only a small number of the members in class discussion. Probably we should not have such big classes, but if we do, the teacher is largely limited to the lecture method. It is also helpful if most of a class do not have the ability or background for lesson study.

It is especially valuable with certain doctrinal studies, and those from difficult portions of the Old Testament. Likewise it is helpful in giving the pupil the benefit of the rich resources of a teacher. Think of the opportunity of sitting under the instruction of a Mullins, Sampey, Robertson, or Tidwell! Also it enables a teacher to present a lesson in a more comprehensive fashion than is possible with questions and discussions, and there is less likelihood of getting sidetracked. And it is possible to come to an inspirational climax not otherwise attainable, which has distinct value.

On the other hand there are several weaknesses in the method. Probably the greatest is that pupils generally will not study. If they know they will not be called on, they are likely not even to read the lesson, much less make any effort to master it. This is true even with seminary students. The writer once taught a Sunday school class of men, meeting in a downtown theater, and found that only one of the sixty-three present had even read the lesson. Of course their minds were not prepared for the class period.

Also the teacher has little chance to find out whether or not his teachings are being understood and therefore to correct error. On an examination once a teacher got three different answers to one question, any one of which being true, the others would have to be false. He had been misunderstood, but would never have found it out during a lecture. And, then, the pupil does not learn without mental activity, and this is often reduced to the minimum by the lecture. Too often the pupils merely "sit still while the teacher instills." So the method has its disadvantages as well as its advantages.

2. *Discourses of Jesus*

The lecture method, or didactic discourse, was used considerably by the Teacher especially during the first part of his ministry when he dealt largely with the multitudes. Sometimes it was given to large crowds and sometimes to small ones. Sometimes only the disciples were present, and at other times the masses or a mixture of the two. "His pulpit was the hillside or a boat moored by the margin of a lake. His auditorium the blue canopy of the skies, His audience the multitude gathered about him with faces upturned in eager attention who hang upon his life. . . . They call him 'a teacher come from God.' " [1]

Horne lists about sixty of these discourses delivered to the multitudes only, to the multitudes and the disciples, and to the disciples alone.[2] They were delivered in the Temple and synagogues, in cities and the country, in the mountains and by the lakes. The subjects range all the way from wealth and divorce to the sabbath and missions. In line with John's statement that the world could not contain all the things Jesus said, it is likely that we do not have recorded anything like all his discourses, or even all of those that are mentioned.

Three of his addresses occupy more than one chapter and are probably the most outstanding. One is on the last judgment comprising two chapters (Matt. 24-25),

[1] Burrell, D. J., *The Wonderful Teacher*, p. 13, Fleming H. Revell Co., New York, 1902.
[2] *Jesus the Master Teacher*, Ch. 10, The Association Press, New York, 1920.

and setting forth the conditions that will obtain at the time of his second coming, the suddenness of it, and the judgment to follow. Included are the stories about the barren fig tree, the talents, and the wise and foolish virgins. Another is the Teaching on the Mount which occupies three chapters and is perhaps the best known of his discourses (Matt. 5-7). Here he sets out the superiority of his teaching over that of the Law and the prophets, the qualities that go to make a kingdom citizen, and the activities of the Christian. The longest of his discourses is the farewell address filling four chapters in John's Gospel (John 14-17). It is a comforting message, telling of the coming of the Holy Spirit, the vine and branch relationship, problems they will face, and ultimate triumph. He closes with his final prayer for them.

All of these as well as the other lectures are thought-provoking and heart-searching, practical and vital. They cover a wide range of subjects, and show thoughtfulness and preparation. They vary both in style and method. They attracted attention and stimulated interest so much that "the crowds were astonished at his teaching" (Matt. 7: 28). Even those who were unsympathetic went away saying: "No man ever spoke like this man" (John 7: 46). They were moved by his messages. When the Master lectured, the people listened and learned, were informed and stirred, and their lives were enriched. His lectures covered the three-cycle movement of intellect, emotion, and will. The method with him stands out alongside that of the story. In fact stories constitute a considerable part of a lecture.

II. Questions

The catechetical, or question and answer, method is one of the oldest and most prevalent teaching methods. Socrates was famous for it. It was used extensively in both Old and New Testament days and has been practiced ever since. It is one of the most widely used methods of teaching today. As we shall see Jesus made considerable use of questions in his teaching.

1. *Purposes and Traits*

The meaning of the word "catechize" is to sound down, as a sailor takes the soundings to find the water's depth. It may be a haphazard performance with questions asked at random, or it may be an orderly arrangement of queries to bring out the lesson truths. With Socrates it was a systematic means of eliciting information from the pupil on the assumption that knowledge was inborn. The question method is as old as the human race, as nearly universal as teaching itself, and is adapted to all age groups, particularly the Junior and Intermediate departments. We shall never be done with it.

Questions are used for several purposes. For one thing they help to get and hold attention. The pupil, who will go to sleep or let his mind wander during a lecture, will be more alert under questioning, for he does not know but that his time may come next. The element of surprise enters in. For another thing questions help to provoke thought. If they are the right kind and asked as they should be, the pupil is led to think. And this is indispensable in teaching since there is no learning without mental effort. Mere reception of truths, without thinking about them, does not develop the pupil much.

Likewise questions help to clarify and deepen impressions. As one answers a question he is not only led to think, but also to express himself, and by these means truth is implanted since thought and impression both help to deepen it. Rhetorical questions are particularly impressive. And, too, questioning enables the teacher to find out whether the pupil is understanding or retaining what is being taught. So he can check on his teaching, clarify it if needed, and do more efficient work.

In order for these results to take place, however, certain traits must characterize questions and questioning. For one thing they should be clear. This means simple, short, and to the point. The pupil should be able to know what they mean. They should not be like the pastor's question that contained 222 words, or that of the Sunday school teacher who asked: "Who chased whom around the walls of what?"

Also they should provoke thought. Mere factual questions are not enough. Such may be answered mechanically as a pupil did who had been absent; when asked where he was the past Sunday, he replied in line with the first question on the location of the lesson: "Twelve miles northeast of Jerusalem." And they should be asked so as to keep the attention of the entire class. This means as a rule asking the question before calling the name of the one to answer; not repeating a question if one is not listening; calling on the pupil more than once during the class period; and asking questions of interest to the entire group.

2. *Instances from Jesus*

One of the first pictures we have of the Master, after his birth and infancy, shows him asking questions. At the age of twelve when left behind in Jerusalem by his parents, he was found in the Temple "seated among the teachers, listening to them, and asking them questions" (Luke 2: 46, Moffatt's translation). This tendency seems to have stayed with him throughout life. *The Sunday School Times* has stated that he asked 154 questions. Others claim that more than 100 different ones are found in the Four Gospels.

A considerable portion of the written records is made up of questions and answers, and the contents would be changed tremendously were these left out. He depended much on this method. W. P. Merrill says: "He came not to answer questions but to ask them; not to settle men's souls but to provoke them; not to make life easier, but to make it more educative."[1] And Marquis adds: "Our Lord had a habit of throwing in a question now and then that broke up the serenity of his class and made them sit up and think."[2]

In beginning a teaching activity Jesus used questions to attract attention, to get a point of contact, and to prepare the mind for what he was about to say. An illustration of this is found in the query to the disciples: "Who do you say that I am?" (Matt. 16: 13-15). It aroused deliberation about him, started them to thinking, and prepared the way for revealing himself as the Son of God.

Similarly when James and John asked for the privilege of sitting on his right and left hand, he began his teaching by saying: "Are you able to drink the cup that I drink, or to be baptized with the baptism with which I am baptized?" (Mark 10: 35-40). So he prepared them for his answer and almost made them answer their own request. When he said to the rich young ruler who inquired as to the way of life, "Why do you call me good?" (Mark 10: 18), he was evidently preparing the young man's mind for the searching answer he was to give him regarding what constitutes the good life.

Many questions were used by the Teacher in developing his teaching. In fact this was his main use of them. They were of various kinds. Sometimes they were to secure information as when he said to James and John when they requested a favor, "What do you want me

---

[1] Quoted by Horne, *Jesus the Master Teacher,* p. 51, Association Press, New York, 1920.
[2] *Learning to Teach from the Master Teacher,* p. 29, The Westminster Press, Philadelphia, 1913.

to do for you?" (Mark 10: 36). Sometimes they were
to help the questioner think through his own problem.
When the critics of Jesus looked on in an accusing manner as he was about to heal the man with the withered
hand on the sabbath, he said: "Is it lawful on the sabbath to do good or to do harm, to save life or to
kill?" (Mark 3: 1-5). Questions were used to clarify
and even illustrate his teaching. When the Pharisees
complained that the disciples plucked corn on the sabbath, the Master quoted in question form the instance
of David and his followers entering the Temple and eating the "bread of the Presence" unlawfully (Mark 2: 23-
28).

Likewise questions were used as arguments. One of the
classic instances of such use is the statement, "If God
so clothes the grass of the field, which today is alive and
tomorrow is thrown into the oven, will he not much
more clothe you, O men of little faith?" (Matt. 6: 30.)
It is an argument from the lesser to the greater. Even a
question using the dilemma was resorted to in order to
carry his point. When the chief priests and elders questioned his authority to teach he asked: "The baptism of
John, whence was it? From heaven, or from men?"
(Matt. 21: 25). They were silenced, for they could not
answer either way without getting into a predicament.

It is difficult to separate questions for emphasis and
argument from those for application and exhortation,
but it does seem that Jesus used some primarily to emphasize his teaching. As he finished the story of the
good Samaritan, he said to the tantalizing lawyer,
"Which of these three, do you think, proved neighbor
to the man who fell among the robbers?" (Luke 10: 36).
It was a hortatory as much as an informational question.

Similar was the question made to the disciples
which required no answer, "For what does it profit a

man if he gains the whole world and loses or forfeits himself?" (Luke 9: 25). No statement could be as emphatic as that question. Somewhat of the same order was his threefold question to Peter, "Simon, son of John, do you love me more than these?" (John 21: 15-17). He was driving home the exhortations to "feed his sheep." So questions were indeed, "near the heart of the teaching methods of Jesus," and as McCoy points out they were always practical and never theoretical.[1]

III. DISCUSSIONS

One of the most talked-of methods today, especially for grown people is the discussion. It is felt to be particularly adapted to college students. It, also, had a place in the teaching activity of the Master Teacher. As found in his teaching it does not have all of the characteristics of the formal discussion method as defined today, but the essential principles are there.

1. *Nature and Values*

The discussion method is a reaction from the formal methods of storytelling and lecturing in which the teacher does all of the talking, and the recitation method in which the pupil merely gives back from memory the materials of the lesson. In these one may not understand the lesson involved. It has been defined as "the process of arriving at an interpenetrated conclusion through group thinking," and therefore involves a grasp of the truth. It is different from haphazard talking in that there is a plan and purpose. The class moves forward progressively. It differs from propaganda in that one is seeking to find rather than merely promulgate truth. He has an inquiring mind, And it is unlike debate in that there is an effort to appraise rather than

[1] *The Art of Jesus as a Teacher*, p. 127, The Judson Press, Philadelphia, 1930.

discount the view of another. If found to be true, it will be accepted. It is a joint search for truth with teacher and pupils working co-operatively at the task.

Several things are necessary in order to have a situation conducive to an ideal working out of the discussion method. There should be a group of about the same training and interests. Ordinarily a class composed of senior high school or college students will be the best suited for it. There should be a good deal in common not only as to the level of training, but also as to common interests, for normally the topic for discussion will be some personal, social, or religious issue of common concern to the group. It is necessary also to have an open mind for receiving truth from whatever source it may come, for weighing it impartially, and for accepting that which is worthy. Naturally it is important that data be available on which students may draw in their search for material to use in forming their conclusions. Of course it may be used in a modified and fairly satisfactory form without these ideal conditions.

In carrying through the discussion method the teacher becomes more of an inspirer and guide than of an instructor. He is not the star performer but the power behind the scene. He does not so much give out his views or get back those of an author, as he leads the class in arriving at conclusions of their own. So it is his business to help the class select from the lesson material a problem of vital interest, locate sources of information on it, direct in the securing and presenting of this material to the group, assist in weighing and evaluating the information brought in, keep the discussion moving and to the point, and finally see that a conclusion is reached. Naturally it takes considerable ability and training to do these things properly. This, of course, presupposes more of the ideal situation than is found in the average class, so imposes some limitations.

It will be seen from the above statements that the discussion method has a number of very distinct values. It necessitates activity as no other method does. This is involved in selecting a topic, and finding and evaluating material, and contributes greatly to learning. Initiative and creativeness are likewise included, and are very valuable both in the learning process and in developing character. They mark the difference between creative and transmissive education. The social motive is utilized, each feeling that he has a part in the program and a contribution to make, for it is a process of intellectual sharing. Interest and effort are maintained in a splendid fashion. Investigation and evaluation are engaged in, and thought and appreciation are developed. Of course the method has its handicaps in that it is not adapted to all ages or conditions, all types of lessons, or all kinds of teachers. But it is near the top, and on the whole is probably the best single method for mature students.

2. *Illustrations from Jesus*

In the complete and formal sense as above defined, it can hardly be said that Jesus used the discussion method. In fact he hardly used any method in as formal a way as we do. In principle and in the essential elements, he did utilize it. In fact it runs through most of his teaching. However, it was usually with one person rather than a group, and when used with a group it was in a greatly simplified form. Probably the most striking instance was that of dealing with the Samaritan woman at Jacob's well, which has been discussed already. All through this teaching he was leading her on in her thinking, getting her views, giving her his, and helping her to see and appreciate the truth he presented, and to respond to it. It is a fine example of the conversational method which is the discussion limited to one person.

Another good illustration is the Master's teaching of

Nicodemus (John 3: 1-21). He was a Pharisee, a ruler, and a teacher. Raymond Calkins likens him to a "university professor, a judge of the Supreme Court and a bishop of the church." [1] This gave him a legalistic, cultural, and more or less professional attitude. For some reason he came to the Teacher at night and with a complimentary and noncommittal sort of approach.

Immediately Jesus raised the problem of spiritual experience, telling the cultured leader that he must be "born anew," if he was ever to see God's kingdom. This was foreign to his formalistic religion and he thought the Teacher referred to natural birth. Then Jesus told him that he must be born both naturally ("of water") and spiritually ("of the Spirit") saying, "That which is born of the flesh is flesh, and that which is born of the Spirit is spirit" (v. 6).

The Saviour mildly rebuked Nicodemus for being a teacher and unable to understand, and went on to enlarge on the idea, stressing God's gift of himself in order that "whoever believes in him should not perish but have eternal life" (v. 16). Other records indicate that he responded, defended Jesus before the Sanhedrin, and after his death brought linens and spices to help in his burial.

Still another instance of conversation-discussion is that of dealing with the rich young ruler (Mark 10: 17-22). The young man was educated in the Jewish law, had great possessions, was a member of the synagogue, and yet with it all was not satisfied. So he confronted the Master on the road, knelt before him, and asked what to do to inherit eternal life. The problem was raised. The Teacher tested him out by telling him to keep the Commandments. The young man responded that he had done so from his youth. Then discerning the heart of his difficulty (covetousness) he said to him, "Sell all

[1] *How Jesus Dealt with Men,* p. 38, Abingdon-Cokesbury Press, New York, 1942.

that you have, and give it to the poor, . . . and come, follow me" (v. 21). However his feeling of the value of his possessions outweighed his sense of the need of Jesus, and he went away sorrowful. It was the great refusal. But the Teacher let the young man make his own choice. So whether with a debased woman, a covetous man, or a self-righteous leader, the discussion method filled a prominent place in his teaching.

Other methods besides these discussed might be mentioned though they were not as outstanding in Jesus' work. As previously indicated, he used the observation or demonstration method in helping remove John the Baptist's doubt about his being the Messiah (Matt. 11: 2-19). In fact one writer puts most of the use of objects and dramatics under this head.[1] He used the project principle of learning by doing when he sent out the disciples to witness and heal (Matt. 10: 1-42), and later when he sent the seventy on a similar mission, and received them ba'k for a report (Luke 10: 1-12, 17). So they learned as apprentices both by observation and practice how to preach, teach, and heal.

Even an element of the outline method is suggested in the orderliness with which the Teaching on the Mount and other didactic discourses were planned and presented. Therefore in the teaching ministry of Jesus we have in embryo, if not in full development, practically all of the methods used today. He was master of all and greater than all. "Back of the words, the gestures, the methods, was Jesus himself."[2]

[1] Jent, J. W., "The Pedagogy of Jesus," p. 11f, Unpublished thesis, 1912.
[2] Smith, Robert Seneca, *New Trails for the Christian Teacher*, p. 219, The Westminster Press, Philadelphia, 1934.

TEACHING AIDS

I. Lectures
  1. Strength and weaknesses
  2. Discourses of Jesus

II. Questions
  1. Purposes and traits
  2. Instances from Jesus

III. Discussions
  1. Nature and values
  2. Illustrations from Jesus

TOPICS FOR DISCUSSION

1. Why has the lecture method become unpopular?
2. Which was Jesus' greatest discourse? Why?
3. What are some dangers in the question method?
4. Quote the Master's first recorded question.
5. Mention other discussions than those given.
6. Did Jesus use any method not mentioned?

CHAPTER IX

Results of His Service

THE RESULTS of Jesus' work not only show his superiority as a teacher, but also justify his emphasis on teaching. He is indeed the peerless teacher, and stands completely in a class to himself. This statement is true from whatever angle we view it. His followers not only total more than those of any other religious or secular teacher, but also the effects produced in the life of the world have been greater. "Boussett was not exaggerating when he said that practically every forward movement of mankind during the past nineteen hundred years can be traced to Jesus as its main source." [1] We will notice briefly only a few of these achievements. Many more could be given.

I. PERSONALITY EXALTED

Until Jesus came certain groups of people did not have standing as individuals. They were mere cogs in machines, servants of others, means to ends. They were not regarded as personalities with rights on their own account. This was and is one of the supreme problems of civilization.

Henry C. King has well said: "Reverence for personality is the ruling principle in ethics and religion; it constitutes the truest and highest test either of an individual or a civilization; it has been, even unconsciously, the guiding and determining principle in all human progress; and

---

[1] Quoted by Squires, W. A., in *The Pedagogy of Jesus in the Twilight of Today,* p. 57, George H. Doran Co., New York, 1927.

in its religious interpretation, it is the one faith that keeps meaning and value for life." [1]

In Jesus' day the scribes, Pharisees and Sadducees looked with contempt on the publicans and sinners, considered themselves too good to associate with such people and criticized him for doing so. Gentiles were regarded as aliens and heathen, unworthy of the blessings of God, and outside the pale of missionary endeavor.

Jonah was not the only one who did not want to see other people saved. The Jews would not even have dealings with the Samaritans. Women were virtually the servants of men, often were expected to go with their faces covered and keep quiet in public, and in some sections girls were given in marriage by their parents without their consent. Children were not considered as having rights of their own, and weak children, especially girl babies, in some territories were deserted and left for wild animals to destroy. Certain social groups were looked upon as inferior, and the Negro then, as often now, was regarded merely as "a hewer of wood and a drawer of water."

The Master's teachings, however, served to change these attitudes. "Jesus recognized and emphasized the value of man as no other teacher has ever done." [2] He refused to condemn the woman taken in adultery, and taught one of his greatest lessons to the fallen woman at the well. He portrayed true brotherliness when he pictured the Samaritan rendering aid to an injured Jew. His teaching put woman on a par with man, and started the influences that have resulted in woman suffrage and officeholding, and the right of women to participate in church and denominational activities. He set the child in the midst as an example of humility, restrained the objectors who did not want children to come to him,

---

[1] *The Moral and Religious Challenge of Our Times,* p. 1, The Macmillan Co., New York, 1917.
[2] Hitchcock, A. W., *The Psychology of Jesus,* p. 173, The Pilgrim Press, Boston, 1907.

showed the awfulness of putting stumbling blocks in their way, and initiated the influences that have put them at the heart of education.

Jesus' teaching led to the conception that God is no respecter of persons, that "brown and yellow, black and white all are precious in his sight," and that no one has a right to own another. The parable of the prodigal son showed God's concern for persons. Jesus' teachings have brought reverence for personality which is at the basis of all right dealings among men. Persons and not things were put first.

II. LIVES TRANSFORMED

Jesus said that he came to set at liberty those that were bound. Regeneration was at the very heart of his task. The bondage of sin must be broken and the soul set free. This liberating and transforming of lives stands out prominently in his work. Peter was changed from an impulsive, unsteady character into a steady, dependable person. John was transformed from a hotheaded youth into a lovable old man. James was formed into the stuff out of which martyrs are made. Matthew's character was made over. Paul the persecutor became Paul the promoter. Zaccheus a money-grubbing tax collector became "the first Christian philanthropist, giving half of his wealth to the poor, and restoring fourfold anything wrongfully taken." [1] A fallen woman was changed into a home missionary. These and others were transformed, and sent forth. "Eleven re-made men marched with his spirit for ever and a day, into countless millions of battles for the truth of God . . . , eleven of the greatest benefactors of the human race." [2]

What was true of these whom he taught during his

[1] Eddy, Sherwood, *Maker of Men*, p. 21, Harper and Brothers, New York, 1941.
[2] Mead, Frank S., *The March of Eleven Men*, p. 23, Grossett and Dunlap, New York, 1932.

earthly ministry is equally true of those since his death who have been influenced by his teaching and by his spirit. Through the centuries there has been a living and continuous chain of transformed disciples that have continued to shape the destiny of the world. Augustine was changed from a passionate sinner into a zealous Christian, and through his teaching and writing influenced Christian thinking for centuries. Abelard caught the Teacher's spirit and through his teaching at the University of Paris, made Christianity a thinking religion and paved the way for the Reformation. Luther got more clearly his ideas, and as teacher, writer, and leader crystallized the Reformation and turned the tide of civilization.

Space will not permit one to tell of Comenius and Moravian education, Robert Raikes and the Sunday school movement, Francis Clark and the young people's work, and others like Wesley, Moody, and Kagawa. These transformed characters have indeed "subdued kingdoms, wrought righteousness," and changed the course of history. Their lives demonstrate the transforming power of the indwelling Christ.

What they have done under the leadership of God, those whom we teach may also do. From our classes may come changed personalities to bless the world. Little did the old Presbyterian elder realize when he took a Sunday school class of five incorrigible Junior boys and patiently taught them, that someday one of them would be a physician, another the president of a college, another the governor of a state, still another the moderator of the Presbyterian General Assembly of America, and one a foreign missionary. His teaching changed lives and set going influences that have girdled the globe. By the grace of God so may ours. "There is no limit to what may be accomplished by one man absolutely surrendered to the will of God."

III. REFORMS STIMULATED

While it cannot be said that Jesus himself was a social reformer, yet it can be said that his teachings and attitudes have brought about the great moral reforms of history. As these teachings have permeated human life, they have caused people to see that certain evils were wrong, and should be abolished. So, indirectly rather than directly, he has brought about society's greatest reform movements, which after all is often the very best way of accomplishing the end. The emancipation of womanhood, the recognition of the rights of childhood, and the stress on the worth of personality regardless of color, have to some extent been reform movements, and they certainly owe their inspiration to the teaching of Jesus. We have gone a long way toward breaking down the class and caste spirit, and helping people of all classes and colors to become brothers. Even a world war levels differences and binds various groups together.

But his teachings have led, also, to the inauguration of certain definite social reforms. The Reformation grew largely out of the recognition of the rights of the individual, and the desire to break the control of the church over the state so that one might be free to think and act for himself. Slavery was abolished only after William Lloyd Garrison, Harriet Beecher Stowe, and others stressed the Christian emphasis on personal liberty, and public sentiment reached the point where civilization would no longer tolerate one person holding another in bondage.

Prohibition came about after Sunday school teachers had taught quarterly lessons on temperance for a generation, and humanity came to the dual realization that anything which hurts the body harms the soul, and that society is held responsible for putting temptation in the way of its citizens. An effective organization for

world peace will be established not through political diplomats around a peace table, but through Christian
teachers in all lands, teaching citizens in Sunday school
and public school the sacredness of human life. Every
great reform movement has had its inspiration in the
teachings of the Master.

What has been true in the past will continue to be
true in the future. Prohibition will return and be effective only when the Sunday school teachers of America
grow a generation of voters imbued with the temperance ideal. The encroachments of the state over the
rights of the individual in economic matters will be
curbed whenever the citizenship realizes that freedom
is endangered. Immorality will be curbed only as teachers
stress its evils and the need for purity. And as W. J.
Bryan said: "The charter of a league of nations will not
be worth the paper on which it is written unless it is
backed by the spirit of Christ."

IV. INSTITUTIONS IMPROVED

Prior to the coming of Jesus the home was held in
rather low esteem. Outside of Judaism it was very bad,
parents having almost complete authority, and children's
rights disregarded. Moses, on account of the people's
hardness of heart, had permitted a man to divorce his
wife on practically any ground. With the Teacher it
was not so. Due to the nature of marriage he regarded
it as an indissoluble bond and allowed divorce with
legitimate remarriage on one ground only, that of
adultery. Thus the institution was lifted to a vastly
higher plane through his teachings. And it will come
up to that level, and divorces will be curbed, only when
Christian teachers lead the rising generation to recognize
the sacredness of the home and the marriage vow.

Formerly the state was looked upon as an end in itself—an all-powerful institution with complete authority

over its subjects. It was so when Jesus came, especially by the heartless Roman emperor. It has been true in recent years in Nazi Germany, Fascist Italy, and imperialistic Japan, and millions of lives have been sacrificed in breaking down the conception. It exists to a considerable extent in our own land with the government's trend toward "stateism" and regimentation.

But with the Master it was not so. He taught that man was not made for the sabbath or for any other institution. He denounced regimentation by the scribes and Pharisees with their regulations too hard to bear. The growth of democracy (the rule of the people) throughout the world has been due to his teaching, and its continued spread and preservation will depend on the extent to which his teachings are made regnant in mankind. The teacher is the true guardian of society, and the progress of civilization depends on the battle between schoolmasters.

In the parable of the talents Jesus showed that all should work. At another time he said that the laborer is worthy of his hire. And he taught that true greatness is dependent on service rendered. The privileges of the laborer today both in participating in the management of industry and in profit sharing are largely the results of the ideals of the Teacher applied to business. Influential businessmen such as John Wanamaker, Marshall Field, and James L. Kraft have drawn their inspiration from the teachings and spirit of the Master.

V. LITERATURE PERMEATED

The literature of the world has never been the same since the Teacher came. Countless books have been written exclusively about him. Practically every phase of his life has been covered, including his early life and training, his achievements, his teachings, his methods as a teacher, his atoning death, the progress of his cause, his influence on various lines of thought, and many other aspects. The books and magazine articles about him would make a library by themselves. One writer worked up a bibliography on material about Jesus and found more than 5,000 books and articles bearing on some phase of his life and work.

Languages have been reduced to writing to carry his words. No other person has ever filled such a large place in the literature of the world. Some of the books about him have been among the best sellers. This foremost place in the world's literature is all the more striking when we remember that he himself seemed indifferent to authorship, and wrote nothing except a line in the sand. In spite of his having left no written word, he is more quoted than any other writer that ever lived.

One of the most interesting instances of the Teacher's influence on literature is the way in which poets have quoted from him or made allusions to his teachings in their writings. Miss Cynthia Pearl Maus lists 229 in her book *Christ and the Fine Arts*.[1] Much of the poetry of the world's greatest writers is saturated with his ideas. Particularly is this true of Milton, Browning, and Tennyson. The last named said: "What the dew is to that flower, Jesus Christ is to my soul." A large per cent of the 730 poems in *The World's Great Religious Poetry*,[2] by Caroline M. Hill, have to do with him.

Also writers in the fields of theology, ethics, general history, educational history, psychology, sociology, and other fields of thought have drawn heavily on his teachings. Not only have preachers and lecturers quoted from him, but even politicians and lawyers have referred to him to emphasize their points. It is not too much to say that Jesus' teachings have permeated and saturated the writing and thought life of civilization for the past 2000

[1] Harper and Bros., New York, 1938.
[2] The Macmillan Co., New York, 1923.

years. No other teacher can claim anything like such a place in the literature of the world.

VI. ARTS INFLUENCED [1]

The influence of the Teacher on the arts has been about as great as on literature. He has left an indelible and universal impression here. Especially has this been true in the field of music. Around the world composers like Fannie Crosby have spent their lives writing hymns to his name, and people have lifted their voices everywhere in universal praise. Soldiers stranded in far-off isles have found their only contact with natives through words and music of Christian songs. The finest oratorios of Bach, Haydn, and Handel have been written to his praise, and have been sung in cathedrals and over radios to eager listeners to the ends of the earth. No one can calculate the influence of "There Is a Fountain Filled with Blood," "Alas! and Did My Saviour Bleed!" and "Amazing Grace."

Likewise the finest works of the greatest painters have been inspired by Jesus' life, if not actually devoted to the portraying of him. This is especially true of Tissot, Raphael, and Rembrandt, the first of whom gave much of his life to painting scenes in the life of our Lord. These paintings have had tremendous teaching value themselves since most of our knowledge comes through the eye. Who can estimate the influence of such as *Christ and the Children* by Plockhorst, *The Crucifixion* by Van Dyck, and *The Last Judgment* by Michelangelo. Even motion pictures are being produced at heavy cost to set forth the Master's life and work while on earth. Take him out of the paintings of the world, and art would be barren indeed.

Jesus' influence on architecture is scarcely less notice-

[1] For more detailed studies see A. E. Bailey's *The Arts and Religion*, The Macmillan Co., New York, 1944; and Cynthia Pearl Maus, *Christ and the Fine Arts*, Harper and Bros., New York, 1938.

able, especially as related to the great cathedrals. This
has continued throughout the history of Christianity.
Styles have changed from time to time in harmony with
the changing conception of the church and its work, but
always they have been in the direction of beauty, gran-
deur, and service. The most beautiful architectural
structures erected through the centuries in various nations have been the cathedrals built for the worship of
Christ. Notable among these have been Rheims, St.
Peter's, and Westminster Abbey. Likewise sculpture
within and without cathedrals has been influenced by
him. Catholics have always made much of the images
of Christ, especially his crucifixion. But it has been carried much further in some cathedrals and we find extensive carvings such as that of *The Last Judgment* in
Bourges Cathedral in France.

VII. PHILANTHROPY INSPIRED

While Jesus owned nothing himself, apparently failed
to get the rich young ruler to distribute his wealth, and
severely condemned those who sought riches, he has suc-
ceeded in a marvelous way in inspiring owners of prop-
erty to give it for the needs of man and the spread of
the kingdom. Says Sherwood Eddy: "Jesus possessed
no wealth. He owned nothing at his death save a seam-
less robe. We have no record that he ever asked for anything for himself on earth save one drink of cold water
which was denied him. He possessed nothing, he asked
nothing, he gave all .... Jesus arraigned the wealthy ....
Yet fortunes have been flung at his feet and he, more
than any, motivates and guides the noblest philanthropic
giving of the world today." [1] Men have given away millions because of his example and teachings.

This was true in the early centuries when men and

---

[1] *Maker of Men,* p. 13, Harper and Bros., New York, 1941.

women of wealth sold or gave away their possessions; took the vows of poverty, chastity, and obedience; and withdrew to caves, dens, and cloisters to try to live a righteous life. It has been true in recent years when men like Carnegie, Rockefeller, and Hardin have given much of their fortunes to libraries, schools, and hospitals because the teachings and spirit of Jesus so disturbed their consciences that they dared not die with all of their money on their hands. All along he has inspired people to use their funds to his glory. He alone has led humanity to see that it is better to give than to receive. Society is richer and character stronger because of his stress on giving.

Hospitals and nurses' homes, orphanages and homes for the aged, and Christian academies and colleges, in the homeland and on foreign fields, stem from the philanthropic spirit generated by the Master. And those fostered by states and municipalities indirectly flow from the Christian spirit. In fact it is not too much to say that whatever is unselfish in the government's movement for social security gets its inspiration from the teaching of Jesus that we are to love our brothers as ourselves. He is indeed the master Philanthropist of all the ages. All of us are the beneficiaries of the giving he has inspired.

VIII. SERVICE MOTIVATED

Right along with the spirit of philanthropy comes the motivation for service that leads individuals to forget ease, comfort, and selfish gain and give their time, talents, and energy to help those in need. Inspired by Jesus' example people have left the luxuries of civilization and risked their health and lives to carry his message to those in darkness and depravity to the uttermost ends of the earth. Livingstone, Judson, and Grenfell are striking examples. No one did that for Socrates, Epictetus,

Abelard or any other great teacher. As a result, "Savage tribes have been uplifted, cannibals civilized, headhunters converted, schools and colleges founded, and the character and culture of individuals and of peoples changed." [1] The whole missionary enterprise is a living monument to Jesus' motivating influence. No group of men in history have matched, much less surpassed, the sacrificial spirit of the world's great missionaries.

What is true of the foreign mission enterprise is likewise true of various other lines of service. The Red Cross organization to minister to the sick and needy in times of pestilence and flood, and to the injured and dying in times of war—even the giving of blood itself—gets its motive from the teaching and service of Jesus. Rescue missions in the sinful areas of our cities and social work centers in the slum sections come from the same source. Lives of service given in homes for the aged, orphans' homes, and hospitals for the physically and mentally ill are inspired by the same spirit.

Clara Barton, Frances Willard, and Jane Addams are shining examples of servants of humanity motivated by the spirit of the Master. After observing for a day his son's skilful practice of medicine among the needy and being told regretfully that there was little remuneration in it, a farmer father replied, "Son, I would give anything to be able to serve like that. Go on with your practice. I will go back to the farm and make a living for both of us." When Louis Pasteur, the famous scientist, lay dying, he clutched a cross in his hand and prayed that his discoveries might never be used to the hurt of man. And some of those who helped to develop the atomic bomb have been saddened by their achievement.

Sherwood Eddy sums up: "He was allowed less than

[1] Eddy, Sherwood, *Maker of Men,* p. 9, Harper and Bros., New York, 1941.

three years in which to do his work; little more than a
year in his public ministry, and a year in retirement
training his pathetic remnant. He was cut off in his
young manhood, a little past the age of thirty. Socrates
had taught for forty years, Plato for fifty, Aristotle had
lived long and filled libraries with his learning, Buddha
and Confucius had fulfilled their three-score years and
ten. He was among a crushed people, under an oppres-
sive legalism, zealously opposed and hated by scribes and
Pharisees, betrayed by Jews and crucified by Gentiles.
He left no book, no tract, or written page behind him.
He bequeathed no system, no philosophy, no theology,
no legislation. He raised no armies, held no office, sought
no influence, turned his back forever on might, magic and
cheap miracle . . . , (yet he was) to transform the bigoted
Jew and universalize his religion; to show the philoso-
phizing Greek the highest truth; to win the proud Roman
to plant the cross on his standard instead of the eagle;
to stretch out his hand to the great continents and transform them—to Asia, to savage Europe, to darkest Africa,
to America." [1]

And another adds: "I am well within the mark
when I say that all the armies that ever marched,
all the navies that were ever built, all the parliaments
that have ever sat, and all of the kings that have ever
ruled, put together, have not affected the life of man
upon earth like this one solitary personality." Measured
by any standard he was without any question the world's
greatest teacher. And humbly we are to follow in his
steps, and "make disciples of all nations, baptizing them
. . . , teaching them to observe all that I have commanded
you" (Matt. 28: 19-20).

---

[1] *Maker of Men,* pp. 3, 10, Harper and Bros., New York, 1941.

TEACHING AIDS

BLACKBOARD OUTLINE

I. Personality exalted
II. Lives transformed
III. Reforms stimulated
IV. Institutions improved
V. Literature permeated
VI. Arts influenced
VII. Philanthropy inspired
VIII. Service motivated

TOPICS FOR DISCUSSION

1. How did Jesus transform life?
2. Mention other reforms wrought through Christianity.
3. Contrast the home in Christian and pagan lands.
4. Mention three poems bearing on Jesus.
5. List five greatest hymns written about him.
6. Give other results of the Master's teaching.

FOR REVIEW AND WRITTEN WORK

Chapter 1

1. How did Jesus' embodiment of truth affect his teaching?
2. Show how he was recognized as a teacher.
3. Indicate some things he knew about human nature.

Chapter 2

4. Discuss the impulsiveness of Peter and John.
5. Give illustrations of sinful tendencies in the disciples.
6. What were some of the issues Jesus' pupils faced?

Chapter 3

7. Give scriptural evidences of his meeting life problems.
8. Show the Master's emphasis on character development.
9. In what ways were the disciples trained for service?

Chapter 4

10. Show how Jesus discovered possibilities in pupils.
11. Why did he put ideals above regulations?
12. How did he secure the student's self-activity?

Chapter 5

13. What were the three sources of the Master's materials?
14. State and illustrate the forms used by him.
15. Explain three ways in which he used materials.

Chapter 6

16. Explain the elements in beginning a lesson.
17. Discuss Jesus' lesson development with the Samaritan woman.
18. What is involved in closing a lesson?

CHAPTER 7

19. Give instances of the Master's use of object lessons.

20. What are the values in the dramatic method?

21. Show the three ways in which he used stories.

CHAPTER 8

22. State two strong points and two weak points in the lecture method.

23. Show how the Master used questions in his teaching.

24. Give three instances of his use of discussions.

CHAPTER 9

25. How has personality been exalted by Jesus?

26. Discuss his improvement of institutions.

27. Name some reforms which have been stimulated by him.